DANCING
with a porcupine

Parenting wounded children
without losing your self.

JENNIE OWENS

FOREVER HOMES PUBLISHING | KENNEWICK, WA | 2019

forever homes
PUBLISHING

Forever Homes Publishing
1601 Columbia Park Trail #104, Richland, WA 99352
Foreverhomes.org

Printed in the United States of America
Published 2019 | First Edition

Library of Congress Control Number: 2018911649
ISBN 9781081166519

To inquire about bulk copies of this book, email info@foreverhomes.org or call (509) 713-1004.

Cover and interior design by Sara Nelson Design, Ltd. (saranelsondesign.com)

CONTENTS

Foreword

I remember reading about how each of us must experience the fires of suffering sometime during life. Those of us who have already come through the flames lend an unspoken credibility to those who yet have to enter the fires.

Jennie Owens is one such woman.

Because Jennie and her husband adopted three wounded children whose behaviors remained severe for many years, she has suffered tremendous rejection, Post-Traumatic Stress Disorder, dashed dreams of motherhood, marital discord, and health struggles that almost took her life.

Over the decades, I've read and endorsed many books about adoption, but this one stands apart from the rest. I believe every adoptive and foster parent should read this book. In fact, it should be required reading by CPS and adoption agencies.

So many books explain behaviors of kids with attachment issues, but they leave the reader somewhat in the cold. Bring them into the realities of Jennie's day-to-day mothering, and each how-to becomes crystal clear.

When other adoptive and foster moms read *Dancing With a Porcupine*, they'll realize with Jennie that their home may no longer be a relaxing sanctuary but a place of extreme behaviors rooted in trauma.

Jennie's words are a sanity check for moms at the end of their ropes, who believe they can't possibly continue. She lends the validating and comforting words, "I've been there. I made it through the fires of suffering... and you can too."

—Sherrie Eldridge
Author, *20 Things Adopted Kids Wish Their Adoptive Parents Knew* (Random House, 1999)

Preface

I look back now and wonder how I am alive to tell this story. That I didn't die or lose my mind and end up in the hospital, psych ward, lake, or prison is an absolute miracle. After all, I'd put myself on the back burner for a long time.

Time and time again, I have watched parents caring for children from tough places become so engrossed with their child's pathology that they live their lives on the edge of burnout.

In our minds, if we can just help our child heal, everything else will fall into place. But it's dangerous to become so focused on the quest to help a child heal that we neglect ourselves in the process. Far too late, we realize the toll putting off our own care has taken on our bodies, relationships, emotional and mental stability, and our very lives. Our self-neglect sabotages the helping of our children.

It was hard to go back into those dark times in order to write this book. Yet through those times, I learned that no matter how dark the journey gets, there is always hope. Healing didn't always fit my expectations or follow a straight path, but it came.

I tried to infuse this story with humor, but parts may be difficult or disturbing to read. Despite that, I hope it encourages you.

To those parenting a child with extra challenges: you are not alone. If the trials and challenges sound familiar, this book can offer you hope — you can survive, no matter how hard it seems at times.

To the rest of you: I hope to give you a better understanding of what these families go through. I hope you're encouraged to walk alongside a family that is working through hard times.

— Jennie Owens

Acknowledgments

• To my husband, Lynn, for patiently supporting me and challenging me to pursue what God has called me to do.

• To my mom, who has always encouraged me in life and in my talents and has been there for me through thick and thin. Thanks for helping me with editing, too.

• To my dad, who taught me the value of working hard and showed me how to persevere.

• To Angie Konitzer, who encouraged me to write this book.

• To my children, who have taught me so much along the way and have shown in their lives the power that love and faith have to radically change a life.

• To those of you who walked through this with me. You know who you are. You are my tribe. Even if your name doesn't appear in this book, my appreciation for your love and care does.

• To Sheila Bender, Molly Hollenbach, Kevin Cole, and Sheila Gibbons for walking alongside me in the writing and editing process.

• To Sara Nelson and Kevin Cole of Sara Nelson Design for all of their design work, support, and encouragement. Without them, this book wouldn't have made it to completion.

• To Elizabeth Brown, who introduced me to the idea of "dancing with a porcupine."

Introduction

"Relationships are hard," my mom said, without further explanation.

I was sitting on the time-out chair in the dining room of my childhood home. My sister was planted firmly on her own chair at the opposite end of the hutch. Mom returned to the kitchen to finish making dinner.

We were supposed to be facing forward, but every so often I would glance to the side to see my sister's tongue slip out of her mouth ever so slightly. She was always better than me at not getting caught. We were fighting moments earlier over a board game. I was seven and she was four.

I often desperately believed that life was unfair, and the world was tilted in favor of my sister. Every time I felt angry toward her, she would make me laugh. I tried to ignore her, but eventually she would wiggle her ears or cross her eyes, and a giggle would escape me.

My mom would warn from the other room, "That's enough, girls. Finish your time out, and you can go back to playing." Part of me wanted to stay mad at my sister forever, but as I glanced in her direction she smiled again, and I knew I wanted her as a playmate more than I wanted her as an enemy.

"Relationships are hard," my mom sighed when I came home crying in fourth grade because my best friend made a new best friend.

Carolyn was in the "gifted" class. Her classroom was adjacent to mine. I felt shame that I wasn't deemed gifted and spent my days looking longingly into the unknown world of the kids whose futures were more promising than mine.

At first, it wasn't a big deal that we were in different rooms. We saw each other at recess and walked home together at the end of each day. As the year wore on, she had different classroom assignments and special field trips, and I felt envious.

One day, I was waiting for her at the flagpole in front of the building to walk home. She was usually there first, so I looked around in surprise. Finally, I saw her about half a block down the road, walking with someone else. I squeezed back tears and began the walk alone. I watched as she turned off at her driveway and waved to her new friend.

The tears unleashed, and I ran the rest of the way to my own kitchen table, where I was met by the sympathy of my mother. I wanted to crawl under a rock and never return to school again.

My parents encouraged me to call Carolyn and tell her how I was feeling. They practiced with me a few times and then left the room so that I could stretch the phone cord as far into the dining room as it would go. I started by asking her if I had done something wrong. She responded that I hadn't. We talked for a few more minutes about school, her new friend and the sadness I felt. She apologized and invited me to join the two of them on the playground the following day.

It was difficult to widen my circle of friends, but the difficulty was worth it.

"Relationships are hard," my dad nodded as he stiffly patted my back.

A school bully had been slipping handwritten threats and insults into my locker at the high school. The girl didn't like that I had refused to move from "her" seat on the bus.

The weeks that followed were filled with anxiety as I was afraid to open my locker or enter the girl's bathroom alone. She followed me in the hallways whispering curse words under her breath.

I stood my ground, and my dad was proud. "Keep it up, Kristin. You are doing the right thing." It was difficult, but the more I ignored this girl, the stronger I felt. Her threats lost power over me and I began to see her insecurity seep through the cracks in her exterior.

My fear turned to sympathy and my sympathy to compassion. I ignored her invitations to fight, and after a month she let it drop. I never formed a friendship with her, but I was able to walk the hallways of my school with my head held high.

"Relationships are hard," my mom soothed. "There are plenty of fish in the sea."
I hated that statement.

I was 16, and my boyfriend had just dropped me like a bad habit. I hadn't seen it coming, and I seriously thought that our eight-week romance was true love. I lamented that I wouldn't have a date for prom.

I draped myself dramatically across the living room couch until my mom told me to shake it off. "I know it's tough, but you just have to get back out there. Don't let him know this got to you. You are pretty, smart, funny, and kind. The right guy will come along one day." I sighed and squeezed out a few more tears, "You have to say that because you're my mom!" She rolled her eyes, "That's true, but the stuff I said was true, too."

I did end up finding the right "fish" eventually, and we've been married for many years.

"Relationships are hard," my dad said, "but don't quit. Marriage is worth it." Then he squeezed my hand just before walking me down the aisle to my groom.

He was right. Marriage has been tough. Sharing a home and a life with someone is challenging, but also comforting, fun, joyful, and safe. It took years to get into our groove as a couple, then as parents and now as business partners.

When I adopted my first child, I looked into her warm brown eyes. I felt her tiny fingers wrap around mine.

My heart filled with love, and I thought this relationship could never be hard. It would be filled with unconditional love — nothing else. I went on to adopt seven more children, and with each addition, I thought the same thing. I believed I was born to be a mother. I knew I was going to shine at this role. I forgot about my own humanity and the humanity of my precious children. I almost forgot that relationships are hard. All of them.

Within the pages of this book, Jennie tells a story of a difficult relationship. She tells of her own hurting, her own successes, and her own failures. She tells a story that we all know in some way: Relationships are hard, but be encouraged; the tough things are also the most rewarding.

— Kristin Berry
Co-founder, confessionsofanadoptiveparent.com

CHAPTER 1

You're Going to Die

"If you don't get rid of your stressors, you're going to die," the doctor stated matter-of-factly.

"I CAN'T get rid of my stressors. They're adopted." I chuckled under my breath and looked up. She did NOT look amused.

"Two years ago, my husband and I adopted three children from foster care. They've experienced traumatic pasts, so they have a lot of issues and extreme behaviors that are stressful to deal with. Those are my main stressors, so there's nothing I can do about it."

"Well, you're going to have to figure out a way," she said.

Something in her eyes took me aback. I sat there, staring at the floor and then at her horn-rimmed glasses. Die? I was too tired to ask why she'd said something so dramatic. Her assessment seemed a bit extreme, and I tried to dismiss it. I wasn't quite sure what to think of the slightly disheveled woman sitting on the other side of the desk.

As she spoke, I let her words roll around in my head and soon realized she wasn't far off. Anyone looking at me could tell I wasn't doing well. The person staring back at me in the mirror seemed more like a character in *The Walking Dead* than the vibrant person I once was. Who was the crazy lady looking back at me? The one yelling at her kids, tempted to "hug" them tightly around the neck?

At only 37 years of age, I could barely walk across my small kitchen without getting winded and having to sit and rest. I weighed more than I ever had in my life. I was constantly forgetting things. My brain was in a fog. I turned from Dr. Jekyll to Ms. Hyde at a moment's notice, and I was close to a nervous breakdown.

And the exhaustion! I never knew a person could experience that level of fatigue and still be alive. Having to muster the strength of Hercules just to get off the couch, I plodded through each day. I caught every flu bug or head cold that came my way, and I was waking up six to eight times a night, never feeling rested. I didn't have the energy to care about anything.

I walked out of the doctor's office in a daze.

Get rid of my stressors?

I let my twisted sense of humor roam. The only way I could imagine ridding myself of stressors was to commit three counts of first-degree murder. While three square meals a day prepared by someone else and a room to myself sounded heavenly, prison wasn't the fix I was hoping for.

Decrease my stress?

Brianna and Stephen, biological siblings, had come to live with me and my husband, Lynn, two years before. Bri was now twelve and Stephen was ten. Parker, eleven, arrived six months after Bri and Stephen. Despite my husband's and my extensive training, experience and preparation, parenting these kids for the past two years had proven way more challenging than anyone could have prepared for.

I thought back to my first conversation with our kids' therapist a year earlier.

"I feel like I've been in a war zone," I'd said. It was the only way I could describe it.

She said, "You have."

Olympic Parenting

While I had been fighting on behalf of my children for two years, trying to help them heal, their behavior toward me at times made me feel as though I were battling against them. Their past taught them not to trust, so they pushed away anyone who would get close enough to hurt them. From day one, I had been the primary target of the kids' rage.

I heard that parenting one severely traumatized child was equal to parenting ten typical children. I'd begun to tell people that parenting wounded children was like running in the Olympics instead of a high school track meet. I would never have said it out loud, but I thought it made typical parenting look like eating an ice cream cone on a sunny day in a beautiful meadow.

That Lynn and I became Olympian parents was surprising. Our biggest fight before we got married was how many kids we would have and whether we would adopt. I didn't want to adopt and wanted only three children. On the other hand, Lynn thought it would be great to have a whole brood of biological and adopted children. He loved watching shows like *Cheaper by the Dozen*. "Doesn't that look fun?" he'd say. I thought he was crazy.

At the same time, it wasn't a surprise that God turned my heart toward adoption. According to my mom, at the age of five I told her I was going to start an orphanage. And during every trip to the store, all the dolls "wanted to come home with me."

Lynn and I met while I was working at Life Promotions, a nonprofit organization where I had the privilege of working on Lifest, a music festival that drew more than 20,000 people each year, and Power of One, a youth event attended by over 6,000 students and leaders.

Lynn was a Middle School Pastor at a large church in the area. Prior to that, he had worked for five years with criminal offenders at a boys' ranch in New London, Wisconsin. There he experienced everything from having a teenage boy throw a table on him — then grab a knife and threaten to kill himself — to transporting an extremely combative teen to a lock-up facility.

We met in October, were engaged in December, and married in June. I joined Lynn in middle school ministry for a couple of years, until we felt God tugging at our hearts to work in a group home facility. After a careful search, we discovered a group home in Palm Beach Gardens named Place of Hope, where we helped open a shelter-care house for foster children.

Becoming a Mom

Looking back, I realize that "it" happened during our time at Place of Hope. I didn't know what it was, but I knew it hurt more than I could explain. Through hours of wiping these boys' tears and seeing the effects of abuse they had endured, something stirred deep within me. It was as if my heart was walking outside my body, following each of these young boys.

Never had I experienced anything so unsettling. I had always cared about people, but this new level of caring left me feeling raw and vulnerable. I described the experience in an email update to family and friends. Sheri, one of my sisters-in-law, wrote back and explained it well.

"Congratulations! You've become a mom."

There was no mistaking it. In those first months at the shelter, I became a mom. The children became mine. They invaded my heart, and their lives meant something more to me than a statistic or an idea.

The second little boy to enter the shelter, six-year-old Stephen, eventually became our son. Sporting super hero footed pajamas, a big, toothless smile, and a broken pinky, he had barely entered the house when he meted out instructions:

"I'm going to need a toothbrush, and toothpaste, and soap and... what are those little sticks with puff balls on the ends? I use them for my ears. Q-tips? I'm going to need Q-tips, and..."

It saddened me to see how matter-of-factly this child spoke about making sure his needs were met. He was a survivor, used to taking care of himself. Looking down at his bright, blue eyes and freckled face, I immediately felt a connection to him.

Stephen's sister, Brianna, was two years older and lived on campus, three houses down, in one of the homes for girls. They were removed from their parents when Stephen was born with drugs in his system. Brianna and Stephen spent six years in and out of foster care, often separated for long periods of time. Mom, on another drug binge, would leave them to fend for themselves for days on end. Dad, drunk or high, abused the kids.

Place of Hope worked hard to bring Stephen from a boys' shelter in another city so he could live closer to his sister.

100,000 Kids in Need

Before working for Place of Hope, I had no understanding of the need for quality foster care homes or adoptive homes for legally free foster children. Few people ever talked about foster care.

There are more than 100,000 children in the United States who are unable to return to their biological families and are waiting to be adopted. Most of these kids are older, medically fragile, or part of a sibling group. By the time a child turns nine, their chances of being adopted are extremely small, typically because of their behavioral (or other) challenges.

Each year, more than 20,000 youth age out of the system. Statistics predict a bleak outcome for them. They are more likely to end up in prison or homeless than to finish high school. By age 22, only 54 percent will earn a high school diploma or GED. By 24, nearly 60 percent of the boys will be convicted of a crime. In California, more than 70 percent of those who spend time in the State Penitentiary have been in foster care.

We felt God calling us to change the outcome for at least a few children. We loved the kids at Place of Hope, but we wanted to make a more permanent impact. It didn't look like Stephen and Brianna would be returned home, so we called the social worker to let her know we were interested in adopting them if it became possible.

The court date for their mom and dad to lose parental rights was nearing, so the kids' social worker approached them to see if they'd be willing to voluntarily sign over their rights. They agreed. Their mom knew us and liked the idea of having contact with her children, even if it meant receiving only sporadic pictures. She knew that if she lost her rights, she'd have no guarantee of any future contact.

Getting Ready

Our original plan was to work at Place of Hope for another four years to save enough money to buy a house, but instead we left to move closer to Lynn's family in Washington State for added support. We moved in with Lynn's sister until we could find a home of our own and my parents could bring us the rest of our things.

As soon as we arrived, we jumped into the process of becoming foster parents, attending the 27 hours of mandatory foster parent training. I looked over a list of possible poor behaviors we could expect. We'd experienced many of them at the group home, but I wrote off the more severe ones.

"Surely the kids wouldn't do THOSE things!"

After all, we were a strong couple. I was sure our love would overcome any obstacles for these precious children.

We took eight hours of training in First Aid/CPR/HIV, sent in background checks, had fingerprints taken, and filled out towering mounds of paperwork. We labored over an intrusive 13-page personal information form.

Having completed the licensing paperwork, we turned our attention to finding a rental home. Searching high and low, we finally found a nice, clean, three-bedroom home close to a park and middle school. The landlord had recently lowered the rent because he hadn't received a call for weeks. The day after we settled on renting the house, he was inundated with calls from other people wanting it.

After we got the house set up, we stood nervously as the social worker went through our home, inspecting everything for potential safety hazards. We also spent time talking with her as she delved deeper into the questions we had answered in our paperwork.

The process of becoming foster parents was exhausting, yet nothing else mattered as we trudged on, wondering when the day we anticipated would finally come.

Forever Homes

Along with adopting, we envisioned creating a nonprofit organization to train and support foster and adoptive families. The intensive training we had received at the group home helped tremendously. We knew families weren't adequately prepared for or supported in dealing with the behaviors and needs of severely traumatized children.

We appreciated how house parents at the group home provided such intense support for each other. We had learned much from veteran house parents. Being surrounded by others who understood what we were going through was extremely helpful, and we wanted to recreate that same support for ourselves and others.

As soon as we arrived in Washington, I began the research for a nonprofit organization application, in addition to starting the licensing process. Spending hours at the Washington State University library, I documented the reasons foster and adoptive families needed additional support.

After I compiled what I hoped would be a compelling argument for the IRS to give Forever Homes nonprofit status, Lynn added more information to my research, and we sent in the application.

We would have loved to work full-time for our newly founded organization, but we didn't have the money to do so. Lynn found a full-time job at the Boys and Girls Club doing tech support. It wasn't what he ultimately wanted to do, but we knew the state would not hand children over to a couple without an income.

While Lynn worked, I learned as much as possible about parenting wounded children. I read books, spoke with therapists, searched the Internet and attended any seminar I could.

I learned how deeply wounded children push others away so no one else can get close enough to hurt them again. After being abandoned so many times, they reject you before you have the chance to reject and abandon them.

In an effort to protect themselves, they especially push away the primary caregiver, and he or she becomes the target for their anger. They try to prove they don't deserve love or anything good, because they believe this about themselves.

I would soon learn firsthand just how accurate all this theory was.

CHAPTER 2

The Phone Call

We were licensed to be foster parents by November. Then all we could do was wait.

I hoped for the kids to come to live with us by Christmas. Visions of them joyfully opening brightly wrapped presents kept me anticipating the moment we would get the call.

Christmas came and went, and Christmas presents sat unopened in the closet.

The wait finally ended with a phone call the first week in February.

"Hello?" I said hesitantly.

"Jennie, this is Karen," she said. "Everything is ready for you to pick up Brianna and Stephen, so I'd like to get your travel arrangements set."

A couple of weeks later, Lynn and I flew a red-eye out of Seattle to pick up our kids. We arrived in Florida, exhausted but eager.

We spent the week at Place of Hope's guest cottage, connecting with the kids, their schools, the house parents, and the department, taking care of details and ensuring the children would feel safe traveling with us. The kids knew us at the group home, but hadn't seen us for more than six months. We needed time to become reacquainted.

Finally, we loaded the kids into a rental car and headed out. At the airport, Stephen refused to pay attention to Lynn, at times breaking into a full run in the middle of the airport terminal. I focused on Brianna. She sat quietly, deceptively compliant throughout the entire trip. Later I would discover she was listening to incredibly inappropriate music the whole time. She was also wondering if we would beat them.

After a long and exhausting flight, a drive through the mountain pass from Seattle and a stop along the way to play in the snow, these two sweet children came to live with us.

When we arrived home, the kids squealed as they saw Captain, our Newfoundland dog. Captain had been quite a celebrity at the group home, and they were excited to call him their own. They checked out their rooms, shrieking in excitement as they explored their new home.

The Honeymoon

For two weeks we kept the kids home from school. We enjoyed tickle wars, played capture the prisoner (they loved being chased), built forts, and had an all-family slumber party in the living room, complete with Milk Duds and a large-screen projector showing a movie on the wall.

Lynn took a week off from work, and we tried everything we knew to bond with the kids. We would chase them around, armed with Hershey's kisses we would fire into their mouths. This emerged as their favorite silly game, while *Annie* became their favorite movie. They insisted on watching it over and over, and soon we were belting out *Together at Last* at every opportunity. It made me chuckle. I could see how vastly different adoption was from how it was portrayed in the movies.

The first Friday after the kids' arrival, Lynn and I took each of the kids on a date.

Stephen and I had a blast at Chuck E. Cheese, wearing matching bright, lime green shirts Stephen had chosen.

Lynn took Brianna to a father-daughter ball put on by a local church. Brianna, who frequently chose to look like a little homeless girl, decided that she would only wear camouflage to the event, despite the 50's theme.

Being a good sport, Lynn walked his date around in brown and green while the other fathers in dressier outfits showcased girls in poodle skirts and costume jewelry.

Brianna refused to dance with him and spent most of the night playing hide and seek with a group of girls that she met. Lynn sat alone at the table in his camo, trying to ignore the confused looks sent his way.

I was encouraged by how quickly Brianna's "homeless girl" routine dwindled. Soon after the father-daughter ball, as we drove down the road, Brianna asked me, "Mom, do I HAVE to wear a dress to your friend's wedding?"

Thinking back to the recent camo scenario, I thought I'd be nice and not force a dress on her. "No, sweetie. You can wear a nice shirt and pair of pants."

Brianna started getting agitated. "But MOM, do I *HAVE* to wear a dress!?"

Confused, I repeated myself, "No. You can just wear a nice shirt and pair of pants."

"But do I HAVE to wear a dress?" It sounded like a plea.

Finally, the light bulb went off in my head.

"Yes, Bri. You HAVE to wear a dress."

"OK." I looked back at her in the rear view mirror. She relaxed back into her seat, a huge smile on her face, obviously glad to have finally heard the answer she wanted.

This was not the last time Brianna tried to get me to force her to do something that she already wanted to do. Countless times, uncomfortable with making a positive choice on her own, she created a scenario where our only option was to give her a consequence that put her exactly where she wanted to be.

Sabotaging her own success at times and keeping herself out of an uncomfortable situation at other times, Brianna complained to others that we didn't give her enough freedom, even though the situation was of her own making.

I could never figure out why she always got in trouble during lunch, which required her to stay in with the lunch staff to clean. I finally realized that she didn't trust herself enough to hang out with friends at recess, so she kept herself perpetually in trouble. That way, she could save face, staying safe with the adults and not having to go out and potentially make poor choices with her peers.

My Little Porcupine

The depth of Brianna's anger took a while to surface. At first, she was somewhat compliant, although we noticed quite a bit of attitude from the beginning.

Once the honeymoon was over, the gloves were off, and the battle began. She wanted nothing to do with Lynn the first few months and communicated an intense dislike for me. Our days consisted of slammed doors, emotional outbursts, looks of contempt, and deep-cutting jabs.

She made sure we knew she did NOT want to be there and did NOT want to be part of our family. I was NOT her mom and there was no way she would ever think of me that way. In her mind, she was there because it was better than being at Place of Hope.

As if in some strange, confusing dance, though she pushed me away, she demanded constant attention and never wanted to leave my side. She walked into the room like an industrial-sized, turbo vacuum stuck in the "on" position. Her neediness drained the energy from the room like a black hole.

Brianna constantly rolled her eyes and flipped her hair like a teenager. I got so used to the eye rolls that I made a joke of it. She'd roll her eyes; I'd playfully freak out.

"Oh my gosh, there's something wrong with your eyes!"

She'd roll her eyes again.

"There it goes again! Look at that!"

Another eye roll.

"I think we need to take you to the hospital. Your eyes are going to pop out!" I'd say with a wink and a smile.

I figured I could either cry or laugh about it, although her rejection frequently made me feel like crying.

Her message was clear: "I'm only here until I turn 18. Then I'm out of here."

It seemed that her plan was to take us for whatever she could get until she could reunite with her birth mom. I was evidently supposed to be her personal genie. My function was to grant her every wish.

Where's My Candy?

When Brianna first arrived, we had a big bag of Halloween candy her group home housemother had given us to keep for her. We decided to keep it in the master bedroom closet, so we could dole it out at healthy intervals.

A few weeks after her arrival, Brianna asked me, "Where's my candy?"

This sounded like a quiz.

"You already know where the candy is, because you took it." I hoped my instincts were right.

Sure enough, the candy was missing from our bedroom closet.

Only days before, Lynn overheard Bri and Stephen plotting to steal the key and break into our only locked cabinet, in which we kept money and everything we had of value. We were able to thwart that plan, but it wasn't long before other items began mysteriously disappearing.

We decided to install a locking handle on our bedroom door.

The kids watched as Lynn installed the lock. "Why are you doing that?" Stephen asked.

"I'm pretty sure you guys know why," Lynn replied.

I hated having to keep a key to my bedroom with me at all times, but it was better than having things stolen. Even with the lock, this bag of candy would not be the last thing stolen from our room.

Other than a few isolated incidents, Brianna was usually the culprit.

It felt as if Brianna were using both stealing and lying to test how observant and smart we were, as if she were asking, "Am I in control here? Can I outsmart you? Or am I safe with you because you can figure out what I'm doing?"

Mom and Dad's Visit

While much more compliant than Brianna, Stephen loudly clamored for non-stop attention, constantly making noise and chattering. He was a touchy-feely kid, with his hands and much of his body constantly touching anyone in close proximity. He loved to put his face inches away from mine, clinging to my arm and breathing the air I was about to take in before I could get to it.

Stephen's attention-seeking behavior became more evident a month after they moved in, when my parents came to visit. The kids had made huge strides in the short time they had been with us, and I was excited for my parents to meet them.

I was aware of Brianna and Stephen's unusual, challenging behaviors, but my parents' visit made them even more pronounced. As we attempted to sit down to dinner, the kids ran around the table like wild banshees, refusing to sit. Their manners, still atrocious, embarrassed me. We couldn't carry on a conversation without having them constantly interrupting and talking nonstop. Seeing them behave more like wild animals than children, I realized even more vividly that my work was cut out for me.

Mom and Dad stayed for four days. My mom, who has the patience of a saint, would later confess that it was three days too long.

At the end of their visit, we took a picture of my parents with the kids. Mom was forcing a grin, and my dad wasn't even attempting to fake a smile. The blood vessels in his neck were about to pop, and his jaw was clenched more tightly than I'd seen in all my life.

Despite the difficulty for them, the visit had an encouraging outcome. Before, Mom had often tried to offer helpful parenting advice when I shared struggles on the phone. She'd say things like, "Well, maybe if you didn't make Brianna clean her room she wouldn't act out so much."

After her visit, all she would say was, "I don't know how you do it."

My parents were now supportive resources and allies. Now, when I described difficult behavior, they knew exactly what I meant. That helped me to know I wasn't going crazy.

It was the first time I felt understood by someone besides Lynn. Even Lynn didn't see how the kids treated me when he was gone. That made my parents more powerful allies for me than he was at times.

Teaching Children to Play

I never anticipated having to teach children to play, but when Brianna and Stephen first moved in, that's exactly what I had to do. They struggled in doing anything on their own. It motivated me to find fun events to go to after school or on the weekends.

Having an event to provide structure took some of the pressure off me. Even going to the park provided a little reprieve, although they still spent most of their time trying to get my attention.

When Brianna and Stephen had lived with us for two months, I took them to a local gymnastics center, determined to get what I thought would be a much-needed break. As we entered, I looked excitedly at the foam pit, ball pits, balance beams, trampoline, gymnastics rings, springboard, rope swing, and mini zip line.

I looked at the other parents, who were all kicked back, reading a magazine or playing on their phones.

Finally! A place where the kids can play while I get a short breather.

After getting the kids situated, I tried joining the other parents. That lasted all of two minutes.

"Mom! Look at me!"

"Come take a picture of me!"

"Mom! See what I can do!"

I looked around. Three, four and five-year-old children contentedly played, while my seven-and ten-year-old kids yelled the moment I looked away, "MOM! MOM! MOM! Watch me do this! MOM! Take a picture of me climbing this! MOM! See me?"

I was exhausted. I had given nearly constant attention for two months. Now, in a place where I had hoped they would be able to entertain themselves, they yelled for my attention the moment I looked away. As I dragged my lips off the ground to engage with the kids, I found myself jealous of the other parents and embarrassed at being the only one having to supervise her elementary-aged children so closely.

What I didn't know at the time was that my children were going through a very normal phase, just not at the typical age.

Emotional Age

Early on, I read about the need for children who had been through trauma to experience bonding activities.

I learned that foods with lactose promoted bonding, which is why we fed the kids sweets like Hershey's Kisses. I spent thirty minutes of "mom time" with each child after school doing bonding activities. Sometimes this included feeding them ice cream, teaching them fun songs they'd never learned, like *Itsy Bitsy Spider*, or helping them express their difficult feelings.

In the beginning, Brianna would refuse to look at me. Since loving eye contact was an important part of bonding, I'd hold ice cream on a spoon until she looked. Instead of waiting long, I'd surprise her by playfully eating it, then quickly grab another spoonful and feed her the next bite.

At bedtime we'd often carry the kids to bed, swinging them around and singing "Rock-A-Bye Baby" on the way to their rooms. The nights we didn't, they begged to be carried.

I knew many of these activities were typically early childhood experiences but didn't think much of it. I practiced the recommended attachment techniques but didn't fully understand the role of emotional development at the time.

Part of the reason they needed those experiences was because wounded children's emotional age rarely matches their biological age. I didn't understand that those younger behaviors were normal and that wounded kids needed to fill in the gaps in their childhood. Through neglect, abuse, lack of stimulation, or in-utero damage, parts of the brain remained underdeveloped and needed to heal. When my kids wanted every moment of my attention or to eat whatever I had, they were acting out their emotional age, which was somewhere in the toddler range. Even if they had their own pancakes, they wanted mine. They didn't want their drink; they wanted to drink out of my cup.

While most of the time it irritated me, I sometimes used it to my advantage. To get them to eat vegetables, I pretended to care if they ate "my" sugar snap peas. If they thought they were taking something I wanted, they gobbled it up.

We even had a joke about the mama bird feeding her baby birds. My kids would chirp at me, I'm pretty sure only half-jokingly. As I ate a sandwich one day, Stephen stood in front of me and began chirping. I decided to have fun with him, so I spit the food into his mouth. After he recovered from the shock, I could tell by the look in his eyes that at that moment, I was the coolest mom on the planet.

She Handed You Her Heart

A couple of months after our gymnastics venture, I was enjoying what precious little free time I had after the kids went to bed. Sitting in a comfy chair in the office area next to the kitchen, I looked up to see a little girl coming toward me down the hallway.

"What's the matter, Brianna?"

A flood of sobs shook her whole body. I pulled her into my lap as the tears streamed down her face.

"I... pht... .pht... miss... pht... pht... pht... my... pht... pht... mom!"

I have never heard such crying. It was coming from a pain so intense I could only imagine what this child was experiencing.

"Oh, sweetheart! I can only imagine how hard that must be for you," I whispered into her ear.

Holding her tight, I rocked her, caressing her cheek and stroking her hair.

The wails of pain lasted more than thirty minutes. She continued to cry for a little while longer, then calmed and decided to go back to sleep.

The next day when I called the kids' Florida therapist, Cindy, to tell her what happened, she gasped.

"Jennie, I have worked with this girl for YEARS. She has NEVER cried! NEVER! Not even ONCE!"

"Really?!"

"Jennie, do you realize what just happened?"

"No," I sheepishly replied, still unsure of what the big deal was.

"This girl handed you her heart on a silver platter."

I wished I had known better how to handle the tender heart that had been handed to me.

Our First Summer

Lynn and I learned early on that to heal, wounded children needed to do something fun every day, even if they didn't deserve it. It could be something as simple as letting them play with Legos or as elaborate as an outing. To help kids attach, I learned that mom and dad should be where the fun is, so I took that to heart.

In addition to fun being beneficial, I found the kids did better when I kept them busy and planned their every moment. With that in mind, I frequently planned a special activity for the kids right after school. Sometimes we played a board game. Sometimes I took the kids to the park, pushing them on the swings or chasing them around. We joined an athletic club with a pool, so the kids and I frequently went swimming after school.

That summer, the kids and I rode bikes everywhere. I usually had a destination in mind, like McDonald's for ice cream cones. Often, we rode to the park.

Because of the abuse they had endured, they were extremely hyper-vigilant — constantly on guard, scanning their environment for anything unsafe. Every bike ride, car trip, or walk began with an intense and panicked, "Where are we going?" and "What are we doing?"

If we were going to do something fun, I'd simply reply, "You don't need to know. Just trust me." Sometimes I would tell them, in hopes of reducing their anxiety. While the hyper-vigilance was exhausting, it seemed to help when I created scenarios where they had to trust I would take care of them and they could see a positive outcome from doing so.

When we were walking, sometimes I made the walk fun by playing follow the leader. I'd walk silly, dance, skip, or wave my arms, and they had to mimic everything I did. I found that playing this game of follow the leader helped the kids with bonding and made the trips more fun. At times, my background in youth ministry came to the surface, and I'd jump out of the car and have everyone run around it when no other cars were around. They would talk about it for hours afterward.

We spent the summer constantly active and doing something: swimming at Aunt Lisa's pool, having fun at Chuck E. Cheese, going for walks, playing a board game, running through the sprinklers outside, and spending time at the library and park. At the park, I would play with them for a while and then attempt to read a book while they played. That usually didn't work since they spent the time trying to get my attention.

I planned out every moment, even though providing an insane amount of structure did not fit my personality. I scheduled the day in 30-minute increments, knowing exactly what I would be doing with them.

At home, I'd set up an art project, have them work on that for a while, then move them on to playing a board game or reading a book they'd checked out at the library on one of our outings. Neither of the kids could read well, so I spent quite a bit of time reading to them. The non-stop activity was exhausting, but keeping them busy seemed to help prevent emotional outbursts.

That summer, we went camping as a family a lot. I loved camping with extended family because we had other people to help watch the kids. We had the extra responsibility of watching them with the younger kids, but at least there were more eyes.

By this time, Bri was getting much better about receiving love and attention. The kids loved playing in the woods with cousins and playing baseball with the uncles and cousins. The boys pretended that the canoe paddles were guns and played army in the woods.

While camping, I had to watch Bri to make sure she was interacting in healthy ways with any male in the vicinity. I watched both kids to make sure they were not going off with another family.

Neither child displayed an ounce of stranger-danger, a trait very common to children with attachment issues. Both kids would walk right up to a stranger and stand very close to them, as if they were family. If we were present, the kids would stand closest to the strangers and as far away from us as possible. Someone walking into the situation would have incorrectly assumed the kids belonged to the stranger's family. It was stressful trying to keep them safe.

Adoption

When Brianna and Stephen first moved in, we didn't force them to call us Mom and Dad. At Place of Hope we were called "Miss Jennie" and "Mr. Lynn," so we allowed them that option.

It didn't take Stephen long to call us Mom and Dad, but Brianna wanted to be clear she did NOT see us as her parents.

That July, as the adoption date neared, I figured I'd better move it that direction.

One day I decided to have a little bit of fun with her.

"Miss Jennie," she said, trying to get my attention.

I pretended not to hear her.

"MISS JENNIE!"

Again, I pretended to have lost my hearing.

"MOM!" she yelled, exasperated.

"Why, yes, Brianna?" I said, looking over at her with a playful smile. "What do you need?" It didn't take many of those silly interactions for her to start calling me Mom.

We finalized Brianna and Stephen's adoption at the end of August, a little over the mandatory six-month wait after they moved in with us. My parents flew in for the festivities and marveled at how far the kids had come so quickly.

"These aren't the same children we met five months ago," my mom said.

Both sets of grandparents went with us to the kids' adoption proceeding and joined us at IHOP to celebrate.

Later that night, twenty-five others came to our house for an adoption party. Lynn led a little ceremony where we gave the kids rings to symbolize being part of the family. We gave each of them a scrabble board, which I had filled with positive affirmations.

After the ceremony, everyone visited, milled around the house, and wrote encouraging notes to the kids, placing them in the wooden mailboxes the kids had painted.

After their adoption was finalized, Brianna and Stephen suddenly seemed to settle in. It was as if they finally felt that they belonged. I was amazed at how much progress had been made in such a short time, and I was thrilled to see the kids respond positively to the idea of adding another child to the family.

CHAPTER 3

Meeting Parker

I will never forget the day we met Parker.

Since Brianna and Stephen came from Florida, they were assigned two social workers: one in Florida and one in Washington. We had grown close to Megan, their Washington social worker.

Megan had been telling me about Parker for months. His case was so dangerous that she couldn't even put his picture on websites that feature kids available for adoption. She brought him up casually in conversation from time to time, and his story pulled on my heartstrings.

My heart also went out to the social worker as she expressed concern as to whether she could find a home for this little boy without access to any of the normal channels.

Lynn and I asked friends and family to pray about the situation. Neither of us realized we would end up being the answer to those prayers.

We had no intention of adding more children to the family anytime soon. We planned to adopt children younger than Stephen, but figured it would be a long time before we would even consider it.

Four months after Bri and Stephen came to live with us, the social worker begged us to take Parker overnight. She was trying to get respite every weekend for him, trying to appease the foster parents and prolong his stay until she could find a permanent family. Reluctantly, we agreed to help.

When Parker walked in I noticed the cheap, old gym shorts that clad his incredibly skinny legs. He wore a slightly dirty t-shirt that looked too small for him.

Though he was ten years old, he looked to be only six.

While his body looked young, his empty and vacant eyes lacked any signs of feeling or life. Without a hint of a smile, his face displayed a scary indifference. I felt as if I were seeing the picture of a kid on TV who'd just perpetrated a school shooting.

The moment he stepped into the house, I whispered into Lynn's ear, "If someone doesn't help this kid, he's going to end up in prison."

Despite Parker's challenging behaviors, two hours into his time with us I began to get that all-too-familiar tug on my heart. Hoping it was heartburn rather than God speaking, I held onto the thought until Lynn and I were alone.

The next day, the social worker came to pick Parker up, and Lynn and I dropped the other two off with Grandma before driving off for our first weekend away since the kids had come to live with us.

"What do you think about Parker?" I acted as nonchalantly as I could.

"I think we're supposed to adopt him." My heart sank as his matter-of-fact tone confirmed my suspicion.

"I thought it was just my compassion running away with me. Are you sure this is God?" I hoped he would change his answer.

Lynn turned toward me, his voice serious yet full of compassion. "Jennie, you know God's voice."

I did know God's voice, but that didn't make this decision any easier.

While I knew in my heart God had asked us to bring this little boy into our home, I kept whining to Him, "Why me, God? I'm already exhausted. Why me?"

Every time, the same answer came.

"Who else, Jennie? Who else?"

"I can't do this, God." I felt like I'd already run a marathon and was being asked to run even further.

"I know, but I can," I heard in a silent whisper.

Some may say that adopting three older, wounded children so close together wasn't the wisest thing anyone has ever done. I would be the first to agree. In fact, if someone came to me and laid out a plan like the one we followed, I would warn them against it. With that said, I can truly say that we were simply following God's leading, despite how utterly crazy it seemed.

Parker Moves In

The first night Parker came to live with us, a family member called Lynn to ask if he'd help with a computer problem.

"Sam needs my help with his computer," Lynn said.

"Wait. What?? You can't leave me alone with this kid on his first night. He's tough."

"You'll be fine. I'll take the other two, so you won't have to deal with them too."

Despite my protests, he took Stephen and Brianna and left me alone with this deeply troubled little boy.

After an already challenging night, I asked Parker to take a shower. Surprisingly, he complied right away. Soon he was in the bathroom with the shower running.

After 15 minutes, I called through the door, "Parker, it's time to get out."

No sound came from inside except the running of the water.

Unsure of what to do, I repeated the same instruction every ten minutes. As the shower ran, I brainstormed possible solutions. What was I supposed to do with a naked little foster boy who, after the night's oppositional behavior, seemed to be taking an incredibly long shower to tick me off?

More than an hour into Parker's "shower," I'm sure he was no closer to having put any kind of soap or shampoo on his body, yet the water still ran.

I decided to call Lynn. "What should I do? He's been in the shower for over an hour."

"Get him out of there!" I could hear the irritation in his voice.

"How? He won't even respond when I talk to him. Can I physically remove a naked little foster child from the shower? I'm not sure what I legally CAN do!"

Within 20 minutes, Lynn came home and immediately went to the bathroom door, mad.

"You have ten seconds to cover your body with a towel," he barked through the door.

After counting down from ten, he opened the door, picked up Parker, who was luckily draped in a towel, and set him in his room. With an hour and a half shower out of the way, Parker was finally out of the bathroom.

That night, lying in bed, I thought, *Well, I suppose I could have done* **that.** I'd been so afraid of getting into trouble. Foster parenting classes don't teach you how to get a child out of the shower.

I Love You Too Much to Argue

Within a few weeks of moving into our home, Parker's behaviors were so extreme that the school had to place him half days in a classroom for behaviorally-challenged children. He spent the other half in the traditional classroom.

At home, he'd follow me around, arguing over ridiculous things.

"Parker, I'd like you to pick up the food you just dropped on the floor."

"Why should I have to do that?"

"Why do you think I'm asking you to pick it up?" I'd ask, returning his question with a question.

"Because I dropped it, but I don't see why I have to pick it up."

"Sweetheart, I love you too much to argue." I'd learned that phrase in the book, *Love and Logic.* I was trying to be patient, but I could feel myself gearing up for the "War of the Worlds" to last the next 45 minutes. "Just do what I've asked you to do."

"But why do I have to pick it up?"

"I love you too much to argue."

Pointing at Brianna and Stephen, he'd say, "THEY don't have to pick it up. Why should I?"

"What did I ask you to do?"

"You asked me to pick up the food, but I don't see why I should have to."

"Parker, I love you too much to argue."

"But why do I have to pick it up?"

At this point, I'd ignore him, hoping the fact I'd begun dusting the furniture would make it clear I was not going to be pulled in to his argument.

"This isn't FAIR!" His volume would escalate as he followed me around the house, practically tripping me by following so close.

"I'm sure this is tough for you, buddy." I tried to ooze empathy but felt harassed.

I'd head toward my room, hoping he'd give up and stop following me.

"But why do I have to pick it up? Why don't YOU pick it up?"

"I love you too much to argue," I'd say for the 180th time, closing the door behind me and leaving him outside my room to scream. I needed to get away for a moment.

I knew that arguing with a wounded child makes them feel unsafe, but what I wanted to say was, "Shut the h@#% up!"

I'd never been one to swear, but I found myself sounding like a sailor in my head. Gradually the words swirling around in my mind had started to slip out of my mouth. My dad called me one day to see how I was doing.

"How's everything going, Jennie?" he asked.

I told him about Parker's ongoing antics.

"I'm so tired of these damn games, Dad!" I said.

"Whoa!" my dad said with a playful laugh. "What's up with the language?

You never used to talk like that."

"Dad, I tell you, these kids will either drive you to drinking or swearing. Be glad I picked swearing!" I said, thankful my parents didn't judge me when I became frustrated or discouraged.

Tough Kid

When given instructions, Parker would insist he did not hear what we'd just said, becoming agitated or starting to yell if we didn't repeat ourselves. If I did repeat my instructions, he'd say, "Thank you for telling me what I didn't already know," his voice oozing with snarky, sarcastic glee.

I'd look over to see a celebratory grin on his face and feel like I'd been had.

Parker insisted we listen to his constant chatter, becoming frustrated if we didn't listen to every detail of a book he wanted to describe. He asked silly questions he knew the answers to and insisted that I answer each time. When I didn't, he either tried to pull me into an argument or threw himself on the floor in hour-long temper tantrums and wailing meltdowns. If I sent him to his room, he threw and kicked things, screaming at the top of his lungs, sometimes for hours. I thought the screaming would never stop.

The most frustrating part of the whole thing was that hour after hour, I endured his tirades; then, as if it were a bizarre, psychotic dance, the second I showed a hint of frustration, Parker would crumble to the ground in the fetal position, throw his arms in front of his face, squeal and wail as if I were about to beat him. It made me so mad that if I hadn't felt like beating him before that, I certainly did then. And then I felt like a monster for wanting to harm him.

Even on good days, I had to limit the number of questions Parker was allowed to ask or they never ended. After he had asked the allotted number of questions, I simply told him he was done and tried to ignore the rest.

The incessant questions were likely related to the fact he was on the autism spectrum — something we didn't discover until he was 17 because it was masked by trauma. Since he was emotionally young, much of his life centered around himself. He may have been trying to connect to us by talking about something he already knew.

During the challenging times, it was only my commitment to God that kept me going. I knew He had called me to parent this child, and I wanted to do what He asked of me, but I was mad.

In the middle of the chaos, I told God, "The LAST time I listened to you, you did THIS to me! I'm not talking to you anymore!" I didn't realize that in doing so, I was cutting myself off from God's power to do the job.

Star Chart

In the beginning, as I saw no change on the horizon, it didn't take long to need something more than relating to Parker to give me a feeling of accomplishment. In the middle of tantrums, constant questions and arguing, it was difficult to continue giving firm, loving structure and nurture.

One day, I looked at Lynn. "I need to get something good out of handling his outbursts well, because right now I don't even WANT to be patient and loving!"

I decided to do a star chart.

Growing up, I loved stickers and star charts. As a child I collected stickers, especially the scratch and sniff kind. At school or church, seeing that gold star next to my name made my heart swell with pride. I loved the sense of accomplishment.

While typical star charts and motivational methods may not work with some wounded children, I created a twist that helped me. The next time Parker was thrashing around, wreaking sheer havoc, I said, calmly and with a smile on my face, "Thanks for giving me a star, Parker."

"WHAT?!" Parker paused his meltdown.

"Hey, Lynn! I just got a star!!" I yelled across the house.

"Cool! I can't wait to get one!" Lynn yelled back.

Seeing that I wasn't getting upset, Parker stopped his fit. Obviously agitated, he looked up at me. "What do you mean I gave you a star? I don't know what this is all about, but I'm going to stop what I'm doing so you don't get anything out of this. I do NOT want you to get a STAR!"

He quickly calmed and pulled himself together.

We continued to use our star chart for a couple of months. When we handled his difficult behavior well and didn't lose our cool, we gave ourselves a star on the star chart I purchased from the dollar store and followed with a reward after collecting so many of them.

In the end, this helped to decrease Parker's poor behaviors and lightened the atmosphere at the house. We weren't becoming as agitated or angry, because we knew we'd be getting something out of handling difficult situations well. This allowed us to respond more calmly and therapeutically.

Most importantly, it caused me to realize that my success in parenting Parker did not depend on his behavior. It came down to mine.

I wanted to be a successful mom, and each time I parented without anger or agitation was a success. Every moment I could look at Parker with loving eyes, patiently redirect him, or provide empathy with his struggles was an achievement. My sense of being a good parent came from loving my child well, despite his response. My success was based on my choices, which I could control, rather than his behaviors, which I could not.

CHAPTER 4

Bath Time

Parker's hygiene habits were so bad the first five months he lived with us that we finally decided to bathe him ourselves, so he didn't become the smelly kid in class. We figured it would also be a bonding experience.

"Parker, I'd like you to go get your swimsuit on. Dad and I never got to give you a bath when you were little, and we feel sad we missed out on that. Plus, we want to teach you how to take one."

Parker got his swimsuit on, excited at the opportunity to have so much attention. We tried to make the bath fun for him, but we also talked through each step with the hopes he'd be able to bathe himself from that point on.

After we finished bathing him, Lynn said, "OK, Parker. We're going to leave the bathroom now. After we leave, I'd like you to take off your swimsuit and wash your private parts just like we did for the rest of your body. Then you can get out and dry off."

About twenty minutes after we'd left the room, a very shy Brianna approached me.

"Mom, you know that thing you did for Parker?" she asked and hesitated, looking down.

"You mean giving him a bath?"

"Yeah," She looked up for a moment, then back at the ground. She moved her foot back and forth, hesitating for a moment before finishing, "Can you do that with me?"

I smiled at her and said, "Sure, Brianna. Go get your bathing suit on and I'll give you a bath too."

Excitedly, she ran to her room to get her bathing suit.

Brianna frequently asked in her own way for these special bonding moments. Early in her time with us, she had asked for baby food. She was excited when I told her the only way I'd buy it was if I could feed it to her.

A few weeks after giving her a bath, Brianna and I were walking through Walmart when I suddenly realized she was no longer beside me. I looked back and saw her standing at an end cap, staring at the bottles. I walked over, hoping to get her attention, but she stared as if mesmerized.

I had read about parents who filled in gaps by feeding their child a bottle, even though the child was older. In some ways it made sense, but it seemed a little too weird. I was about to dismiss it again when I noticed the longing in her eyes.

"Do you want a baby bottle, Brianna?"

She merely nodded, continuing to stare at the bottles.

"OK, but if we get one, here's the rule," I started. She looked up.

"Since I never got to feed you as a baby, I get to feed you the bottle."

"OK," she said, excitedly, looking back at the bottles.

"Why don't you pick one out? And, you might as well pick one out for each of your brothers." I'd continued doing "mom time" with each of the kids after Parker moved in. I figured if they saw Brianna with a bottle, they'd also want one.

All three got excited about drinking chocolate or caramel-flavored milk from their new bottles and seemed to enjoy being held while doing so. Those bottles provided precious moments of connection during mom time.

At first, it felt awkward to have an eleven-year-old girl who was developing early and almost as tall as me sitting in my lap, being fed a bottle. As I saw how much she craved those earlier experiences, I got more comfortable with it.

The kids seemed to thrive through these bonding moments, though Bri still tried

Dancing with a Porcupine

to avert those big, blue eyes away from me, afraid of the closeness of looking directly into my eyes.

Starting Therapy

That February we found a therapist, though I had to drive two hours to Spokane every other week with the three kids to see her. At one early counseling session, I told her, "Parker keeps pushing and pushing. It's as if he wants me to beat the crap out of him."

"He does. It's what he's used to."

Like many children from traumatic backgrounds, Parker attempted to recreate the chaos of his childhood. Many of these children feel odd in calm surroundings. Uncomfortable, they attempt to change their surroundings to match their insides.

Parker seemed agitated when we wouldn't hurt him, and tried harder and harder to make it happen. I imagined his internal conversation went something like, "Come on, lady! What's it going to take to get you to beat me?"

There were times I would have gladly obliged. Not that I ever condoned child abuse, but I began to understand being pushed way beyond your emotional reserves and losing your temper.

One day, after being pushed repeatedly toward the breaking point, I sent Parker to his room and called my husband.

"You'd better call CPS, because I'm going to beat him." I hoped the dark humor would lessen my desire to act it out. I felt like the worst person in the world for wanting to hurt a child.

"That bad, huh?"

"It's terrible! I don't know how much more of this I can take!"

Relating to Parker felt like riding a giant yo-yo. He spent most of the time pushing me away as hard as he could, in any way he could. He made mean comments, frequently saying cutting things as if they were jokes.

Parker made us aware of his anger in passive-aggressive ways, doing things like calling me "Dad" and Lynn "Mom" or hugging everyone but the person he was mad at. He would say, "I love you!" then look at the other parent with a smirk to make sure they knew he was purposefully not saying it to them.

He pushed and pushed and pushed. Eventually, it would get to the point where I had enough.

"Parker, I love you and will always be your mom, but you have been pushing me away so hard that I need to step back and recover a bit before I can continue helping you heal. I'm taking a short break from doing normal mommy things so I can heal and continue being a good mom to you."

The second he sensed me pulling away, Parker became sugary-sweet.

"Oh, Mom, let me get the car door for you. Can I help you with groceries?"

"How are you doing today?"

"You're the best mom in the world!"

The moment I went back to reaching out to him, he reverted to intensely pushing away. I felt manipulated because he seemed to turn the poor behavior on and off at will. The kids' therapist explained that the reason it bothered me was because his behaviors were aimed at controlling others in an attempt to keep his own heart safe.

I wanted to stay pulled back and not engage with him at all. I knew it wouldn't help him in the long run, but it was tempting to take the easy way out. Over the years, it became harder to want to even try to pursue him. By the time he wanted a relationship with me, it was hard to even think about it.

What made it harder was how nice he could be toward others. At home, he mumbled and talked so unintelligibly that we struggled to understand a word he was saying. Then I would overhear him talking with someone at church and not recognize that it was him because he was speaking so clearly.

His therapist finally told him, "Parker, we are only going to respond if you're speaking clearly; otherwise your mom is going to assume that you aren't talking to her."

Eventually, as the therapist addressed his push-pull behaviors, they began to lessen. I wish I'd understood how early trauma causes children to feel stressed around future caregivers.

Homeschooling

That fall, I decided to home school Stephen, figuring that the next year I could home school Bri. Both came to us extremely behind their grade level. Neither could read even short words like "cat." They had learned to adapt to make it look like they were learning, either cheating or faking it. I wanted to help them get caught up.

By November, Brianna's angry outbursts in the afternoon escalated. It seemed related to the fact that Stephen was home while she was not, so one day I kept her out of school and spent some extra time with her. Her behavior improved so drastically that one night I told Lynn, "I want to home school Brianna, too."

"I DON'T think that's a good idea, Jennie. She's tough and I think it would drain you too much to have her home all day."

"Yeah, I know, but look at how much better she did with one day of staying home. I think it would be what's best for her." I gave him my best puppy dog eyes.

"It may be what's best for her, but would it be the best thing for you?"

"I feel like it would take less energy to have her home all day than to deal with her angry outbursts in the afternoon. Besides, she's doing so much better now that I really want to give it a try."

"OK, but I still don't think it's a good idea," Lynn finally said.

At first, Brianna's behavior improved, but that was short-lived. Defiance and bad attitudes resurfaced, making homeschooling a chore. I spent more time disciplining Bri than teaching her. That made homeschooling Stephen harder. Before, Stephen and I had fun working together. Now my attention was divided between dealing with Brianna's anger and helping Stephen, who was compliant and enjoyable, but still very needy and clingy.

Call CPS

I talked to both Parker's regular classroom teacher and the special education teacher about our recommendations for dealing with Parker's triangulation and other behaviors, but only the classroom teacher took any advice. The special education teacher sneered at me, as if I were a dumb parent trying to tell the expert what to do.

By the end of April, Parker had made a complete turnaround in the regular classroom. On the other hand, the special ed teacher couldn't get him to do the most basic of tasks. She started calling me on a daily basis, reporting his choices and comments in a way that seemed to imply I was abusing him.

"Parker said you didn't feed him last night." Her voice dripped with accusation.

"He actually refused to eat anything for dinner," I would explain. "He had to at least sit at the table with us, but he wouldn't eat."

The next day, her voice would bark on the other line, "HE doesn't have a COAT today."

"Yes, I know. I'm so sorry. He refused to take one. I even tried to make him carry it, but I found out later he'd dropped it behind the bushes when I wasn't looking."

"He came to school in *tattered* clothes."

"I'm so sorry. He tries to sneak out of the house with his old clothes. I'm going to have to put away his play clothes so he won't have access to them on school days."

"He had *dog poop* on his shoes today," she growled one day.

My blood pressure skyrocketed, but I stayed calm. "I'm sorry to hear that, but I am sure Parker stepped in the poop on purpose."

No amount of explaining helped this teacher understand my son was playing her like a fiddle. She simply assumed I was a bad mom.

This dance of accusation and explanation continued until I finally had enough. The next time she called, I said to her, "If you feel we are abusing Parker, you need to report it to Child Protective Services. His social worker knows what's really going on, but in the future, please don't call me with accusations."

That week, I demanded that the school pull him out of her classroom. By then, he was settled enough that the regular classroom teacher felt he could handle a full day, and the administration readily complied.

For the rest of the school year, Parker did great. The teacher told us, "I'll take any child you two adopt."

She even decided to move up a grade the following year and allow him in her classroom a second time.

The other two also improved as my hard work paid off. I watched them make huge strides academically. Seeing their faces light up as they grasped new concepts and watching them uncover their gifts and talents was thrilling.

By the end of the school year, Stephen was reading at grade level, and Brianna had gone from hating picture books with short words to soaking up nearly any chapter book she could get her hands on.

The decision to home school helped Brianna and Stephen. But looking back, Lynn was right: this decision sent me into a dark, downward spiral.

After dealing with the kids' behaviors that school year, as summer approached, I could hardly look at them without feeling irritated, let alone provide the emotional support they needed.

We sent them to the Boys and Girls Club day camp program to give me a chance to heal. The kids went with Lynn in the morning as he left for work, then returned with him when he came home. It wasn't the ideal situation for them, but I knew taking this time for myself was important.

CHAPTER 5

I'm Not Doing My Chore

"We're leaving at 3:00 to do something fun," Lynn announced at 9:00 am.

"Children who have their chore done by that time will be able to go. For the rest, Mom will be happy to babysit, but since this is supposed to be her alone time, she will have to charge a babysitting fee."

"I'm not doing my chore," I overheard Parker whisper to the other two, as if relaying some top-secret information.

From time to time throughout the day, he repeated it, to be sure all had heard.

"I'm not doing my chore."

The other two did their chores in less than thirty minutes, one vacuuming the carpets and the other loading dishes into the dishwasher. Parker had been asked to sweep the back porch, which he could have easily completed in ten minutes, but instead he played. When the other two finished, all three played together throughout the morning and into the afternoon.

When three o'clock rolled around, Lynn walked out the door with two very excited kids, giddy with anticipation over the fun they were going to have with Dad.

Click. As soon as the door closed, Parker threw his tiny body on the floor and howled so loudly that I feared the entire neighborhood would hear and come running. Anyone who heard him would assume I was beating the boy to a bloody pulp.

"Couldn't you give me another chance?! I know I can get it done! Can't I please go?! Plllllleeeeeeeaaaaaaaaassssssssseeeee! I BEG you!" He yelled, writhing on the floor as if in tortured agony, between loud sobs.

I was accustomed to this child's wailing fits, but as I sat on the couch watching him on the floor, I decided enough was enough. As he thrashed about the floor, an idea popped into my head.

"You are more than welcome to wail in your bedroom for free," I said calmly, "but I charge extra for children wailing out here in the living room."

We gave the kids an allowance if they did their chores. Parker knew if he didn't have any allowance money he'd have to "pay" by doing extra chores.

The words had barely escaped my lips when the waterfall of tears and ear-piercing screams stopped. My son jumped up from the floor, calm and collected, as if a light switch had been turned off.

I was astounded. That moment made me doubt all other fits. When was he in control and when wasn't he? It was enough to drive me crazy.

With all three kids, I constantly wrestled with wondering which behaviors came from willful defiance and which came from not being capable. One morning, Lynn told the boys not to do their chores because he wanted to leave early that day. Neither boy had done his chore the entire week, but that morning both did.

It was hard to remember that sometimes the defiance was because they had trouble regulating their emotions, which is typical of wounded kids. Like young children, their brains hadn't developed this skill yet. There were times they were truly not capable of doing what I asked of them, due to brain damage caused by trauma, in-utero drug and alcohol exposure, or developmental issues.

I wish I had better understood their young emotional age. Much of my frustration came from comparing them to other children of the same chronological age (or even sometimes much younger). I would look at my kid and think, "This child SHOULD be able to do what I've asked," or, "They SHOULD be able play by themselves for one minute." I had to learn to let go of "should," because many times the kids simply couldn't do what I expected.

As I learned more about my children's emotional age being much younger than their biological age, I tried to picture each as a young child and respond accordingly. It especially helped when their behavior was silly, demanding, or illogical, which it frequently was.

Baby Picture

Parker came to us as a baby, emotionally. That was hard to keep in mind, but certain moments made it clear. At the beginning of the summer, my husband, a talented hobby-photographer, took the kids out one at a time to the back yard to take pictures of them.

Stephen, with his spiked, dark brown hair and bright blue eyes, hammed it up, dancing and posing during the entire session in his typical full-of-energy style.

Bri, who still hid her beautiful blue eyes behind sandy brown bangs, spent the entire time painfully uncomfortable with the attention, attempting to smile without exposing her slightly-crooked teeth.

Parker, with his light brown hair and doe-like brown eyes, soaked up the fact that someone's focus was solely on him.

Toward the end of the session, Parker instructed Lynn, "OK, now it's time for you to take my baby picture."

"What's a baby picture?" Lynn was curious to see what he would say.

"It's where I sit on the ground pretending to be a baby and you take my picture!" Parker thrust his scrawny legs straight out to the sides and reached his arms up toward his dad as Lynn snapped the shot.

Later, the therapist explained Parker was filling in some of the gaps of his child-hood with us in it.

Another precious moment with Parker came when I had taken the kids swimming. While Stephen splashed and played a short distance away and Bri attempted to get some woman's attention, I noticed Parker intently watching a young mom with her baby. Picking up on a longing in his eyes, I held out my arms and ventured to call out, a little embarrassed and afraid to embarrass him, "Come to Mommy!"

Parker's eyes lit up, and he swam over, arms flailing like a small child. "Goo Goo! Ga Ga! Mama!"

I looked around to see if anyone had witnessed this ten-year-old child loudly speaking in baby talk. Looking at his big, brown eyes and sweet face, I realized that if his behaviors weren't so difficult, I could almost think he was a little cherub. I held him in my arms for a little skin-to-skin bonding before he swam off again.

That precious moment with him held me over for a little while. But it also made me feel a twinge of guilt about an earlier conversation.

Parker had shown me a baby toy. "Can I get this, Mom?"

I looked at the toy he was asking me to buy. Sheri, my sister-in-law, brought it to sell at a yard sale we were doing together. We were getting ready for the yard sale, and I didn't feel like dealing with it.

"That's a baby toy, Parker," I replied, feeling irritated. "Right now we are trying to get things ready to sell. Let's not go shopping just yet."

Looking back, not only would I have purchased that toy, but I would have loved to use the ray gun from the movie *Sky High* to shrink all three kids down to babies and start from scratch. It would have helped to be able to visualize them at the emotional age they were, while giving them a second chance at a normal childhood.

I would have given anything for the privilege of knowing my children at those younger ages and protecting them from the trauma they endured.

We had FUN with DAD

"WE had *FUN* with DAD," hissed Brianna through an angry sneer early that summer.

We had just returned from a weekend camping trip at Lewis and Clark Trail State Park. We took both cars, and Lynn privately gave me the choice of driving the nice, newer car with the children or the old Ford Escort carrying the smelly Newfie, whose rancid stench came from playing in a river all weekend.

I took the dog.

I was the last to pull into the driveway, and my daughter met me at the door with those words. Had they represented an isolated jab, I would have been able to tolerate them, but she had been doling out insults like candy lately, finding any way she could to verbally assault me.

After I sent Brianna to her room, I cried into Lynn's shoulder. Between heaving sobs and strings of slobber, I said, "I can't do this anymore! I can't take one more jab!"

I realized this was the first time I shared with Lynn the pain that the kids' behavior caused me, rather than the anger that rose up because of it. I felt myself melt into Lynn's embrace, thankful for a moment of connection.

It may sound crazy that an emotionally stable, confident, grown woman would be so tied up in knots about emotional barbs shot by children. One might think it would be easy to brush off the brutal words and looks of disdain because they were "just kids." At least that's what I thought. I figured a smaller person's words should pack less of a punch.

Something about what abused kids go through makes them experts at reading people. I knew they weren't trying to be hurtful, but it seemed that they spotted my buttons and — like a shark drawn to blood — pushed them over and over.

At times, seeing the hurtful words as shields that they used to protect their hearts helped me not to take it quite so personally. Other times, the put-downs and jabs wore me down because they just kept coming.

With few breaks, there was no time to process my emotions about the kids' hurtful words and actions. The waves of rejection were overwhelming and constant.

After trying to be strong for so long, I struggled to hold it together. Never in my life had I felt so vulnerable.

The next day, I called Cindy, Bri and Stephen's Florida therapist, and described how hard Brianna was working to push me away.

"Why do you need her to like you so much?"

Her question startled me. I hadn't thought about it like that. After a few moments of introspection, I replied, "I guess I'm afraid of what others may think. What kind of mother has a child who dislikes her so much?"

Brianna's rejection mirrored some of my deepest insecurities and feelings of inadequacy. They brought to the surface things I already questioned. Was I a good mom? Was I doing a good job? Was I doing enough? Maybe I *wasn't* a good mom; maybe I *didn't* love my kids enough; maybe *I* wasn't enough.

I don't think I would have said it out loud, but I believed that if my kids liked me, I was being a good mom. Since they communicated their dislike intensely and frequently, that must mean I was a bad mom. Their rejection forced me to reexamine this belief, because when parenting wounded children, a child not liking you is not necessarily connected to your performance as a parent.

Science Camp

That summer, I signed Parker up for a week of science camp. He loved science, and he was smart. I always told Lynn he was either going to cure cancer or end up in jail. At the time, the jury was still out on which it would be.

I forgot to take him to the first day of science camp, as we'd been doing Boys and Girls Club. The next day, I remembered. When I picked him up, he was angrier than usual.

"I can tell you're mad, Parker. What's wrong?"

"I'm mad I missed this camp yesterday."

"I can understand that, Sweetie, and I'm so sorry you missed a day of science camp. I'm sure it's hard to know you could have been here yesterday and weren't. Did you enjoy it today?"

"No."

"Why? Didn't you like the camp?"

"I was mad because I wasn't at the Boys and Girls Club."

"What you're saying is you would have been mad at me regardless of which camp I dropped you off at, because you weren't at the other camp?

"Yes."

"Good to know."

The next day, while the kids were at camp, I called my best friend, Becky, to talk about that conversation with Parker. I often called her for "sanity checks" to make sure my thinking wasn't off. "Becky, was that normal kid behavior?" I'd ask. Or, "Am I having a bigger response than the situation deserves?"

After I told her what he'd said, she replied, "Boy, that's tough. It puts you in a lose-lose situation."

"No matter what I do with any of the kids, there's no winning. I feel like I'm in a psych ward, but I don't know if I should be the psychiatrist or the patient."

Becky laughed. "Well, we've all wondered that about you."

"Seriously, though, I feel like *I'm* the one who's going crazy. I'm dealing with illogical thinking all day long, and it's affecting me. And, quite honestly, the padded walls sound appealing."

"Well, their unhealthy thinking may be affecting yours, but this is not you, it's the kids."

"You're right, but sometimes it doesn't feel like it, which reminds me of what the kids' therapist told me a couple of weeks ago. She said, 'Jennie, you keep trying to make sense of their behavior. There's a reason they call it insanity. It doesn't make sense.'"

"Maybe that's why you feel like you're going crazy. You keep trying to make sense of something completely illogical."

I knew there was more. I needed to put my finger on why I felt like I was losing my mind.

Double Bind

When I got off the phone, I searched online for "lose-lose" and "no-win situation," phrases Becky had used. I came across a term that helped me make more sense of it: "Double bind."

The definition fit perfectly. "A double bind message is where someone sends two or more messages, with one message contradicting the other. Successfully responding to one message means a failed response to the other, thus creating a confusing, no-win situation. In a double bind, the person receiving the message is unable to resolve or leave the conflict, nor can they comment on the conflict."

It made so much sense. Successfully responding to such a situation becomes impossible because you're wrong no matter how you respond. Damned if you do, damned if you don't.

It made me think of an article I had read about a lab experiment. When rats received a shock every time they touched an item in their cage, they stopped touching that item but freely explored the rest of the cage.

Lab rats who received random shocks unrelated to a specific behavior ended up sitting in a corner, huddled and afraid to move. Rather than avoid a specific object, they stopped doing anything. They experienced "learned helplessness."

Many times, I felt like that lab rat. No matter what I did, the kids were angry, and I got "shocked." They acted out and pushed me away if I gave them attention, then acted out because I didn't give enough attention.

At times, when I figured out what my children needed and satisfied those needs, their behavior escalated instead of being calmed. I received messages such as, "I don't want you to be my mom, but don't you dare care about anyone besides me," or, "Go away, but don't leave me." It was confusing.

No wonder I felt like I was going crazy.

I was tired of the anxiety, confusion, and stress the double bind messages caused. I wanted to crawl into a corner and stop interacting with my kids. Why keep trying? I was going to get hurt, no matter what I did.

One day, the kids' therapist challenged me. "You know you're going to get payback no matter what you do, so decide what you want to do and do it. Don't let the kids' payback control your decisions."

It helped me to recognize the difficulty of dealing with a double bind message. I had to learn to stop looking for any kind of affirmation from my children. When I quit looking to them to see if I was doing a good job, I could make a choice based on what I felt was best instead of listening to their conflicting demands.

I had to remember that those conflicting messages came from a place of deep woundedness in my children. They sent the message, "Go away, but don't leave me," because they truly wanted to be close, but closeness frightened them.

I also had to keep in mind that this was their issue, not mine. I was caught in the crossfire of their internal conflict. To keep myself grounded, I needed to connect more with good friends who understood the abnormality of my experience.

Wow. Look at All Those Bathrooms

Late that summer we went to Jubilee Lake for our yearly camping trip with Lynn's family. It was the one place where the kids were able to have fun without being by my side at every moment.

On our way there, Lynn got off the highway and drove down a smaller road. I looked out the window as we passed a Taco Bell, Burger King, McDonald's, and a few gas stations. Seconds later, I heard a quiet voice from the back of the van.

"Wow," Brianna said, wistfully. "Look at all those bathrooms. I bet those are some nice bathrooms."

My husband and I looked at each other and chuckled under our breath.

I turned around to look at her. "Do you need to go to the bathroom, my dear?"

After a sheepish, "Yes," from the back seat, we let out a hearty laugh and stopped at the nearest gas station, making sure she knew we were happy to stop anytime she needed.

Because they didn't get their needs met earlier in life, the kids struggled to know how to ask for what they needed. Especially in the beginning, that meant frequent whining.

Trying to teach them healthy ways to ask, I'd say, "I'd be happy to answer your question when you're speaking in a normal voice," or, "I'm sorry, I can't understand what you're saying. I don't hear whining," or, in my sillier moments, "I'm so sorry, honey. I don't speak Whine-ese." Other times, I'd ignore the whining and respond when they talked in a normal voice.

For the longest time, Brianna would stand and stare at me while I was cooking.

"Do you need something?" I would ask, feeling uneasy.

Brianna would shake her head no.

"Are you hungry?"

"No."

"Do you need a drink of water?" I'd ask, trying to figure out exactly why this staring contest was happening.

"No."

Exasperated, I'd give up and try to fix dinner while an 11-year-old, standing seven feet away from me, stared holes into the back of my head.

One day, we again went through the litany of possible needs. No, she didn't need a drink. No, she wasn't hungry.

Finally, I asked her, "Do you need a hug?"

Brianna meekly nodded yes. Motioning for her to come over, I gave her a big bear hug. Afterward, she went off to play for a short while.

The kids also used lots of hinting to get needs met, which was one of many reasons I hated taking them shopping. While all children hint for treats at the store, wounded kids often take normal behaviors and exercise them to the hundredth degree.

"Oh, what a cool box of cookies."

"I've never had a Butterfinger before."

"I've always wanted to have a scooter."

"I love you, Mommy!"

The last one bothered me the most. While it sounded sweet, it never felt like it was said out of relational motives.

"OK, what do you want?" was my usual reply since it was the only time they said it.

The hardest to deal with was when they demanded something. That made it hard to want to meet their needs.

Both Brianna and Stephen struggled with an unusually large sense of entitlement, which seems to be common in kids who have been neglected and abused.

I had expected it to be the opposite for kids who hadn't had their needs met, but it seemed that they overcompensated by assuming that now they should get anything they wanted. Much of this behavior simply came back to their emotional age.

It was challenging to remember that traumatized children frequently try to get legitimate needs met in inappropriate ways. The needs are normal, but the behaviors are sometimes obnoxious.

I had to remember that fact the week after we got back from a very fun week of camping.

Disneyland Expectations

I'd taken Stephen for a one-on-one outing to get ice cream and go swimming. We had a blast.

The next day he was a wreck, acting out in his usual passive-aggressive manner. He pretended not to know how to do what I asked of him, or acted like he didn't hear me. When he started to obviously try to get in trouble, it tipped me off to his Disneyland expectations.

In general, Stephen was fun to be around, but he struggled with unrealistic expectations. He envisioned every day looking like a trip to Disneyland or a cruise to the Bahamas, with me in the role of cruise director. It got worse after we did something fun together, which made me not want to take him anywhere.

That day, I sat him down and said, "It seems like you had fun with me yesterday, and I'm so glad, because I had fun with you. I can see you're struggling with how today is supposed to look. I'd like you to write down what you expected today to look like. List all the activities you thought we were going to do."

Sitting at the table, Stephen worked on his list. And he worked. And worked.

Thirty minutes later, he came over to me with a two-page list in hand. At the top was "get ice cream" and "go swimming," like we had done the previous day. Below that, he had written at least 100 wonderful activities, like "play basketball," "go for a bike ride," "play Monopoly," "go fishing," and "go to McDonald's."

"OK. Now I want you to plan out what a day would look like if we did all these activities. What time would we get up?"

"Eight o'clock."

"OK, write that down. Now write how long we would do each activity and plan out the rest of the day."

After getting to midnight on his paper, with each activity taking no more than thirty minutes, he had barely made a dent in the list. After we talked about it for a little while, I could see it click in his mind. He laughed at the fact that he had been expecting something of me that wasn't even humanly possible.

After that day, Stephen's Disneyland expectations started to become more realistic.

CHAPTER 6

Parker's Birthday

As summer came to a close, Brianna and Stephen grew excited about going back to public school. I decided that my sanity and ability to help them heal was a higher priority at that time than their academic success. They had come a long way, and I felt that they would be able to continue catching up.

Besides, I needed the break of having them at school if I was going to make it.

As the other two got excited, Parker's anxiety over the start of school increased. Not only was the start of school approaching; so was his birthday.

Birthdays in general were hard for Parker. Other people's birthdays were hard because the attention wasn't on him. He'd be enraged and jealous that someone else was getting presents and he wasn't. On the other hand, I think his own birthday was hard because of his autism. He couldn't handle positive moments and emotions.

The previous year, I pulled up to the school to pick up the kids on the day before his birthday and noticed Parker's teacher standing next to him. I swallowed hard.

As soon as I got out of the car, she looked over at Parker and said, "Why don't you go ahead and get in the car?"

"Please don't bring him tomorrow," she begged as soon as he was out of earshot.

"Why? What happened?"

"He's so anxious he created sheer chaos in the classroom. Based on how he behaved today, I can't even imagine what tomorrow would look like."

"Won't I get in trouble for not bringing him?"

"Trust me, you won't. PLEASE don't bring him!"

The next day, he stayed home with me and I didn't *have* to imagine what that day would look like.

Parker wailed for hours. He asked questions to which he already knew the answer. He argued about everything. He was so out of control that in a rare moment of calm I finally gave him a piece of paper and pen and asked him to plan out how he intended to sabotage his birthday party. His paper quickly filled as he wrote about things like stealing treats from other kids, acting like he didn't know what we'd told him to do, and arguing.

By the time our guests arrived for his birthday party that evening, I was exhausted. As I sat like a zombified mess on the couch, Parker made a complete 180-degree turn and greeted our guests like the perfect host, as if nothing had happened.

With Parker's current birthday behind us, he settled into the school year and seemed to be doing well. In fact, all three kids seemed to be doing well until late September, when we realized that the boys had started injuring each other at night when we thought they were sleeping.

We knew it wasn't safe for them to share a room anymore. My husband and I began a frantic search for a suitable home. Until we could find a house and move in, Stephen slept out in the hallway each night to keep the boys separated.

Parker's Adoption

We found a house and were set to close in the middle of November.

The day before closing, Parker's adoption was finalized — a day he long referred to as "the worst day of my life." His dream of moving back in with his former foster family was now dead.

Inexplicably, Parker expected us to take him to the toy store after the proceeding and let him pick out as many toys as he wanted. I had no clue where he got that idea, but I knew some foster kids tend toward fantastical thinking.

I began to realize that adoption, while a beautiful thing, is also a picture of loss.

I'd read in *The Primal Wound*, by Nancy Verrier, about how even newborn babies grieve when separated from their birth moms. These babies have become accustomed to their mother's voice and heartbeat and they no longer have anything familiar to turn to for comfort.

Newborns can pick out their mom's scent from the beginning. Where is that scent now? Too young to understand the loss, many children adopted at birth never know why there seems to be a hole in their hearts. They just know something is missing.

When I looked back on pictures of Brianna and Stephen's adoption after that, I noticed two things. First, Lynn and I are standing there, silly, wide grins covering our faces, unable to contain our excitement.

Later, I began to see a mix of emotion in the kids' eyes, including fear and sadness, in contrast to our sheer excitement.

Why didn't I realize they were experiencing extreme grief? No matter how much safer they were, adoption was a huge loss for them. Their birth mom wasn't coming back for them.

On Parker's adoption day, there was no question he was angry and sad about becoming a permanent member of our family. He acted out the entire day, even at the big party we held at the Boys and Girls Club. Despite his anger, it was interesting to see that he treated the ring we gave him like a cherished treasure.

The New House

The day after Parker's adoption, we signed papers and began renovating a somewhat dilapidated house my husband found in a neighborhood near his family. The only four-bedroom house in our price range, it had been in foreclosure. We needed to replace the old, urine-stained carpets. Most of the walls had to be refinished; some had to be torn down and replaced. The house needed a fresh coat of paint over the entire interior, and the bathrooms had to be completely gutted and renovated.

We didn't realize what a toll the process would take on our relationship with the kids.

After our offer was accepted, my mom and dad agreed to come out from Wisconsin to help get the house ready. They had built several houses from scratch as a hobby, and we were thrilled to have their help.

They came for the adoption, and my mom helped us for a week before flying home to go back to work. My dad, who was retired, stayed an entire month, stripping down both bathrooms to the studs and rebuilding them, and working on countless other projects.

I worked on the house with my dad while the kids were at school. I left to pick the kids up after school and brought them back to the new house. I'd start a movie for them in an empty room or let them play video games — something we usually didn't allow because of the behaviors that followed.

I kept working, checking in on them as frequently as I could. Lynn joined us after work, and I ran to get dinner for everyone. After dinner, the kids went back to videos.

The next month became a frantic scurry of activity. There were times that we worked on the house until after midnight. On weekends, other family, friends, and a few Good Samaritans we didn't even know joined in to help us.

I felt bad that I wasn't able to give the kids much attention during that time, but we needed to move in by December. I knew we'd pay for the lack of attention in difficulties later. The three could barely handle ten minutes without my attention, so I knew the quiet couldn't last.

Sure enough, while the house was improving, the children were not. Letting the kids play video games and watch movies kept them out of mischief while we worked, but their behavior afterward showed that it wasn't good for them.

By the time we moved in, all three children began to spiral out of control. Parker was so out of sorts that I had to keep him by my side as I worked, which became challenging when I had to paint doors in the garage. The second I wasn't looking straight at him, he'd try to touch saws and other sharp objects to force me to interact with him.

"Parker, I'm talking to you non-stop as I work. That's as much as I can do right now," I scolded, becoming exhausted at not being able to look away from him for one minute.

His behavior had become so difficult to work with over the past month that his psychiatrist prescribed "happy pills," a name we chose because we couldn't make it through much of the day without him taking one.

In all the years our therapist had worked with that psychiatrist, it had been the only situation extreme enough to warrant prescribing that medication.

After watching Parker for an afternoon, Lynn's mom, Sharon, said, "I almost took one of those pills after watching him for twenty minutes. I don't know how you guys are handling this!"

None of the kids handled the move well, partially due to lack of attention, but mostly because the move itself triggered so much past trauma for them.

Foster children tend to be moved frequently, typically having to throw what little they own into a black garbage bag. My children were no exception. All three had been in foster care for about seven years before they'd come to live with us, and they had been moved from birth family to foster families and back again many times. Moving brought up painful memories and feelings of abandonment.

Christmas Eve

That year, Christmas Eve began like most days. Parker sat at his door, waiting with supersonic ears for the turn of our door handle. We made a rule that he couldn't leave his room until we came out of ours, but I regretted not telling him to wait until we came and got him. I laid in bed as long as I could, dreading the moment I had to come out of my room.

It didn't matter how quietly I opened the door. The second the handle turned, Parker was out of his room and in the hallway. As I looked down the hallway at his expectant face, I felt like a gazelle cornered by a lion. I'd soon be devoured by his need for attention.

As he healed, I would describe it to him like this: "Parker, I'm feeling stalked right now," or, "I'm feeling pounced on."

The move, mixed with Parker's anxiety about Christmas, added such an intensity to the mix of his typical challenging behaviors that I could barely take it.

He spent the rest of the morning arguing and asking silly questions like he had when he first moved in. He threw temper tantrums with ear-piercing shrieks that drove me to the brink of insanity, though I'd grown quite accustomed to them.

Lynn went into town to run some errands that morning. Left alone with the three kids, but needing to get ready for the day, I sent them all into their rooms and turned on the chimes that we had placed on their doors for their own safety. I told them not to come out for any reason.

Since Parker loved to wait until immediately after you closed the door of the only functioning bathroom to insist he had to go that very minute, I made each of the kids go to the bathroom before starting my shower.

I no more than turned on the water when the too-familiar tone of his bedroom door chime sounded. Sure enough, there was a knock on the bathroom door.

"I have to go to the bathroom!"

"Parker, you just went and I'm in the middle of showering!" I shouted over the water. "You are going to have to wait until I am done."

"But I have to go to the bathroom NOW!"

"You will have to wait, Parker!" I wasn't even trying to mask my frustration.

Parker went back in his room but was out within a minute to insist once more he could not wait until I was finished. Though my time in the bathroom lasted less than ten minutes, he came out and pounded on the door at least four more times.

"I really have to go!!"

"Go back to your room, Parker!"

Exasperated, I finished my shower and dried off, trying to ignore him pounding and yelling outside the door. I was relieved I had locked the door, a habit all of us had developed because you never knew when he would try to open the door while you were in there. I put my clothes on and opened the door to let him in.

Come Look at My Poop!

Soon Parker came out of the bathroom and made a beeline for me.

"See, Mom. I really had to go! You have to come look at my poop."

"Parker, I am NOT going to go look at your poop!"

"But there's blood in my poop. You *have* to come see it."

"Thank you for letting me know about the blood, but I am NOT going to come and look at your poop."

Moments later, Parker brought out a handful of toilet paper, smeared with poop, and shoved it toward my face. "See! Look! I really did have to go!"

"Parker, I'd like you to go put that in the toilet," I said, as patiently as I could, while I held off a strong gag reflex.

Shortly after, Parker made me aware that instead of throwing it into the toilet, he had wiped it all over the side of the vanity.

Handing him bleach cleaner and some paper towels, I told him I wanted him to clean it.

Parker complied, wiping off the vanity with the paper towel.

He then smeared the poop from the paper towel on the bathroom garbage can.

I had him clean that up.

He did, then proceeded to place the stained paper towels on the floor of the bathroom.

I instructed him to take them out to the garbage bin. He flung them around the yard. By that time, I was done fighting. I left the paper towels outside and sent him to his room for a while. I couldn't take any more.

Parker wailed, kicked the walls and door, and threw things the entire time. The noise and commotion frustrated me, but at least he wasn't out in the living room with me. I figured he was safer in his room than right by my side.

Often when my children acted out, I did a "time in," having them come close and sit with me instead of sending them away in a time out. It helped with the bonding process and didn't cause them to feel the rejection wounded children so easily feel. It communicated that even though they were making a poor choice, I still wanted to be with them. This, however, was not the time to do it.

In more than twenty-five years of working with kids and teenagers, I never once thought of hurting a child. It scared me that this child's behavior made me fantasize about it on a regular basis.

My husband, who had more patience than Mother Teresa, usually fantasized about leaving him along the road somewhere.

Lynn returned from his errands around one o'clock. Then it was my turn to go into town. When I returned two hours later, my husband met me at the door, his eyes bulging and his veins popping out.

"I want to throw him across the room!"

At least it wasn't just me. I entered the house and together we continued dealing with Parker's outrageous antics for the rest of the day.

A Perfect Gentleman

Later that night, we all loaded into the car and drove to my sister-in-law's house for the family Christmas get-together. Parker created sheer chaos in the car the entire way over.

The moment his feet crossed the threshold, however, it was as if he flipped a switch, from rage to perfect gentleman, in an instant. A sweet smile replaced the scowl as he entered the house.

"Can I help you with anything, Aunt Lisa?" he politely asked as he entered the main hallway.

Going from person to person, Parker spread joy wherever he went.

"Ha, Ha, Ha! That's so funny, Uncle Dave!" I watched as he batted his eyelashes, something he frequently did when we met new people.

"Can I get you something to eat, Grandma?"

During the entire party, he behaved like a perfectly charming little boy.

Later, while the conversation buzzed around them, I watched from across the room as he approached Lynn and said, in a syrupy-sweet voice, "Butterfly kisses, Daddy!"

Huskily, Lynn replied, "Parker, you can't treat me the way you did all day long and expect to get all snuggly now!"

The entire room gasped, then became dead silent as they looked at Lynn in horror.

Time stood still for a moment, everyone seeming to wonder how in the world my husband could talk like that to such a darling child; a darling child, who, as soon as we got back home "accidentally" knocked my new porcelain candle holder off the coffee table. He looked down, exasperated, and set it back on the table. He "accidentally" knocked it off again. This time it shattered.

As he spent the night spreading cheer, I walked around in a fog. I remember hearing muffled voices, and I was vaguely aware of others around me, laughing, joking, smiling. After all, it was Christmas. A time to be happy. A time for love and laughter. A time for cheer.

While others excitedly chatted, I numbly sat and stared at the floor like a zombie. The last thing I wanted to do was celebrate anything. I watched the activities around me as if looking through a window from the cold, snowy, outside into a warm home full of happy people. I saw smiling faces around me, but had no energy or inner warmth to engage in anything festive or happy.

After our second Christmas with Parker, it was official: I hated Christmastime.

Barely Crawling

After the holidays, I was thankful for the start of school.

"I feel like I'm supposed to stop doing Forever Homes for now," I said to Lynn at the beginning of January.

The reality was, God had been telling me, in no uncertain terms, that I needed to quit working with Forever Homes for the time being.

"What about all those moms? They need you! And we're in the middle of planning for the benefit concert."

"I know, but I'm drowning. I don't know what to do, but I know I'm doing too much."

Seeing panic in his eyes, I dropped the subject. He was struggling with knowing how to help the moms without me. Forever Homes was on a roll, and he didn't want to leave families in a lurch. He also needed my help in planning the benefit concert we had committed to in September.

Rather than listening to God, I kept going. I took calls from hurting moms, helped lead support groups and provided support to others, while I, myself, could barely crawl.

All three children had settled down tremendously in the past year of living with us, but they spiraled out of control after the move.

I went from feeling like I was in the middle of a war zone to feeling like I had been transported to the depths of hell. I felt more like a prison warden than a mom.

Home used to mean a place of safety and refreshment to me, but it had become a battleground, with lives of three children in the balance.

It was so bad that if I went outside, I had to take the kids with me so that none of them could lock me out.

I couldn't leave anything of mine lying around the house because it would be broken or stolen the instant I turned my back.

I also didn't leave any beverages out. If I forgot to take it with me when I stepped out of the room, I poured it out when I returned. I felt a little paranoid about that, but I didn't want a child to spit in it or worse.

Later, when Brianna had healed more, she confirmed my suspicions as she got me a cup of water.

"Don't spit in it!" I joked.

"Mom, I don't do that *anymore!*"

I lived in a toilet. At least that's how it felt. We lived in a rental when the boys first started urinating out their anger, but there they would only pee in their garbage can or, once, in the kids' toothbrush holder.

In the new house, one of the boys started saturating the brand-new carpets. We had to get them cleaned on a regular basis.

The other built a little "pee shrine," keeping an ever-growing collection of urine-filled bottles under his bed. When we found them, we made him empty them and throw them out, but they kept reappearing. We tried quite a few interventions before the pee shrines and urine-stained carpets disappeared entirely.

The smell was so bad that I tried to hold my breath from the beginning of the hallway, where one son's bedroom was, down the hallway to the other son's bedroom, across the small hall from our bedroom.

Usually I didn't get there fast enough, and the pungent smell reached my nose as I fumbled to insert the key to open the master bedroom door.

CHAPTER 7

Boogers

As I put the groceries away, I looked at the clock and had the sinking realization that in a couple of hours I'd be pulling up to the school. The war on behalf of three angry children would begin again. A sense of dread overcame me.

After I picked up the kids from school and they finished their snacks, we started homework time. To prevent sheer anarchy, I spread out the kids' homework spots. Since the move, Parker had started picking fights with the other kids and trying to hurt them when we weren't looking.

You could always tell where Parker sat. There were boogers wiped all over that part of the table. I figured each one he wiped there meant one less he could wipe on a cup or a bowl.

This latest phase had started as soon as we moved. I didn't know how such a small child could produce so much of the stuff. He would sneak into the kitchen and carefully place a large booger on a cup or bowl.

Every time we pulled something out of the cupboard, we had to hold it to the light and check. Often, we needed to rewash it. He also targeted the faucet, oven and microwave handles, so we had to check before touching them as well.

The day we moved into our new house, fifteen family and friends who helped us move were taking a break, eating pizza. Parker stuck his finger up his nose, pulled out a juicy one, put it on his pizza and proceeded to eat it. I looked around and saw the looks of disgust on people's faces, but no one said a word.

I tried not to let it bother me, but it became hard not to react in disgust. I wanted to gag and throw up every time I saw him do it or when I found one in the kitchen. I felt bad that the other kids had to deal with this issue, although some-times I suspected Stephen added a few of his own to the mix, trying to get Parker in trouble. A lot of animosity had developed between the boys.

Our therapist suggested many ways to help him, to no avail.

After the move, Parker also started behaving like a baby skunk. As soon as I would pull him onto my lap for one-on-one time, a familiar smell would waft up to my nose. Parker not only passed the smelliest gas in all creation, I swear he was able to do it on command. I tried to view it as him protecting himself, but it was still disgusting.

I liked things clean. My husband teased me about being a germaphobe. But between the boogers, farts, and urine, I had to turn off part of my brain and go into "camping" mode to prevent myself from thinking about being surrounded by dirt and mess.

Spinning Plates

Surviving homework time was a feat. Like a man spinning plates in the circus, I worked hard to keep the children from spinning out of control.

After getting Brianna and Stephen going on homework, I turned to Parker. "OK, Parker, it's homework time."

"I don't have any homework," he lied. I knew he had some.

"You know the drill. You have thirty minutes of homework time. You can use that time how you want, but you have to stay at your spot."

After researching how to handle homework, Lynn and I had determined the best way to do it was to give the kids thirty minutes of homework time, during which they could sit and do nothing if they wanted. If they weren't doing well in school, they obviously needed more time for homework and had to spend an hour.

We never forced them to do their homework, but I was always available if they needed help. We learned that if we made their homework more important to us than it was to them, they would try to sabotage it anyway, so it was better for us not to force anything.

Despite our research, I was getting flak from one of Brianna's teachers.

"I just don't understand why a loving parent would not be more involved in a child's education."

"We DO value their education," I replied, trying not to let my irritation show. "I make sure they have homework time every day, and I'm available to help them if they need it. I read with each of the kids for 30 minutes each day."

"I think you should sit with her and make sure she does it."

How? Am I supposed to move the pen for her?

Despite the push-back, we stuck to our original plan. We found that it helped the kids take responsibility for their actions. They didn't like having the consequences they got at school for not having their homework done, and eventually it paid off with both Brianna and Stephen.

Stephen was almost to the point where he didn't need a set homework time to do his work. Brianna still needed guidance and homework time, but she started to care about doing well in school, though it didn't always reflect in her grades.

Parker started doing better at his schoolwork before the move, but afterward he had a lot more trouble. Sometimes, like Brianna, he would finish his homework but refuse to turn it in at school.

"OK, Stephen, you're good to go with homework? Need any help?"

"Nope. I've got it." It was nice not to have to worry much about him doing his homework.

"I'm going to do reading time with Bri, so I'd like you guys to keep working until it's your turn." I needed to verbalize expectations constantly to prevent home-work time from coming apart.

Bri and I sat on the couch facing the dining room for our thirty minutes, so I could see exactly what the boys were doing. I especially had to watch to make sure Parker was not harassing Stephen, although Stephen occasionally doled it out as well.

Stephen had to go to the bathroom. Parker, as he often did, insisted he also needed to go to the bathroom, so as soon as Stephen had gone into the bathroom, Parker pounded on the door. I instructed him to wait, and, surprisingly, he didn't have any meltdowns.

I noted that many of Parker's frustrating behaviors centered around the bathroom. The week before, he had broken the toilet seat, so it slid around when someone sat on it.

On the way back from the bathroom, Parker interrupted Brianna's reading time.

"Parker, you know the rule. Sit over there until it's your turn." The next time he interrupted, I ignored him, and eventually he went back to his seat.

Stephen tried making noises to get my attention but stopped after a quick, "Knock it off."

I'd finished reading with Brianna. "Stephen, are you still doing OK?"

"Yep!"

I got Bri going on her homework and turned my attention to Parker.

"Parker, it's your turn."

Parker soaked up reading time, never wanting it to end, because my focus was solely on him. Eventually it had to end, and his homework time was finished, so he went into his room to play with Legos. I loved that he was back in his room, so I didn't have to supervise him as closely. From where I sat in the living room, I could see if he came out. Everything was so central in our new home that I could supervise the other kids while still seeing how Parker was doing.

"I'm Bored!"

After I'd read with Stephen and homework time was done, I would put out activities for the kids to do, changing the activity every thirty minutes. I'd set out a puzzle or an art project, or let them do Claymation, something Lynn had taught them the summer before. We wouldn't allow them to do video games or solitary screen time, because it made their behavior worse.

I didn't have to be quite as structured as when Brianna and Stephen first came to live with us, but I still had to structure their time much more than I thought I would by this point. If I didn't constantly interact with them by introducing new activities, it didn't take long for things to go south.

While he demanded a lot of attention, Parker could at least entertain himself for short periods of time with Legos or Sculpey art clay. In fact, he was a talented artist who used Sculpey to make life-like recreations of video game characters, down to Bowser's tiny, sharp teeth or Mario's bushy eyebrows.

Bri and Stephen, even after living with us for two years, still struggled to entertain themselves and couldn't do anything without me right beside them.

If there was a lull in activity and I sat on the couch, they'd sit next to me, one on either side, clamoring for my attention. If I told the kids to find something to do, they sat by my feet.

"No, this is not finding something to do. Find something to do," I'd say, irritated at not having any personal space.

Stephen would move away a little bit and play with Legos on the floor. I had been thankful Parker taught him how to play Legos and he could at least do that for a while. He usually only did it when I insisted he do something without me.

Bri would sit across from me on another couch, pretending to read a book. While her eyes were on her book, I could feel her focus like a laser beam boring a hole in my head. She'd pounce as soon as I looked her direction, jumping back next to me on the couch and attempting to get my attention, with Stephen shortly in tow.

A couple of months before, I sat down with the kids and brainstormed a list of possible activities for when they were bored. My hope was that they'd look at the list and find something to do on their own.

Even with that list, the only things Brianna could come up with were to take a nap, bath or shower.

I was thankful that at least by then all three kids had learned not to say the "b" word. After hearing that word way more than seemed normal, I'd begun to help them with their little problem.

"I'm BORED," they'd say.

"Oh, sweetheart, I am here for you," I'd say with a playful grin. "I have something you can do."

They never liked my solution, as it always involved some sort of work around the house. After complaining a few times about being bored and being made to do chores, they'd start to say, "I'm b-".

"You're what?"

"Never mind," they'd say, running off to find something to do before I gave them a task.

Impromptu Therapy

Increasingly rude behavior from Brianna let me know it was "therapy" time. Most days included "therapy" for each of the kids, regardless of what fun adventure I had planned for the day. I made sure I could see both boys before pulling her into my lap in the family room.

"I can tell you're angry about something. Use your words, not your actions."

I'm sure the kids got just as sick of hearing us say "use your words" as we were of having to say it. "Use your words" became a mantra in our home. It was repeated so often that when my husband and I were on vacation and ran across a mug with those exact words, we bought it. If a child acted out their feelings instead of talking, we would sometimes set the mug in front of them as a reminder.

Bri was growing in her ability to use words but had a long way to go. I usually had to play dentist, "pulling teeth" to get her to talk about anything real. It took a lot of work, and there were times I didn't have the strength to pull any longer.

"You played a GAME of CLUE with me yesterday!" she growled.

"OK..." I started with an inward sigh.

Again I found myself trying to be patient but feeling frustrated at the all-too-common damned if I did, damned if I didn't paradox. On the other hand, I was proud of her. Sharing her feelings took a large amount of courage for her.

"Why did it bother you so much?"

Her eyes teared before she pushed back the emotions, only to have them well up again without her permission. We sat in silence for a few minutes. "Because I wish my birth mom would have been the one playing with me." I could barely hear her whisper.

Looking into this child's eyes, some of my frustration melted away. My heart felt heavy, breaking once again for the pain she had endured.

"Bri-Bri, I can only imagine how hard it must be. You must miss her a lot."

While outwardly I validated her feelings, there was always a bit of a sting when she talked about wanting to be with her birth mom instead of me. I understood her pain, but it was especially hard when I was the one drying her tears and dealing with the misplaced anger because her birth mom wasn't there for her in the first place.

Brianna nodded.

"What do you miss most about her?"

"I don't know."

"What things did you do together that you miss?"

Brianna looked up, as if searching for the answer on the ceiling. I listened to the grandfather clock my dad had built, ticking as I waited for her answer. "Um... she took me shopping."

"Yeah? That's great! How often did you guys go?"

"Well, she usually took me shopping after she'd been gone a few days from doing drugs."

I held back my shock and asked more questions, trying to get her to open up about other good experiences she'd had with her mom. It saddened me that much of her hesitation came from the fact that she couldn't remember doing anything fun with her mom. In fact, the biggest reason she wanted to be with her mom was because she was worried her mom would die without her being there to take care of her.

Looking into the face of my hurting little girl, I pushed back the tears. While Bri struggled to come up with another activity she had done with her mom, she did remember something her mom would say to her, which seemed to bring her comfort: "I love you higher than the sky, deeper than the ocean, and more than the stars."

Grieving

Sometimes I struggled to recognize and validate the kids' grief, but it became obvious over the years that they needed to talk about those important people in their lives. While I viewed their parents as people who'd abandoned or hurt them, their sadness made it clear just how personal grief was.

From time to time, Bri and Stephen would talk about their birth parents or grandparents. One of their fondest memories was eating from the mango tree in the back yard when their family lived with their grandparents. Their grandma would freeze the mangoes, and the kids would enjoy this delicious, frozen treat on a regular basis. Bri remembered putting it on Frosted Flakes. They also talked about how their dad always put a surprise candy treat in the bottom of their ice cream cone.

Their sad and scary memories tore me up.

Bri told me she stood at the end of the driveway for nearly her entire birthday party one year, waiting for her birth mom to come like she had promised.

Stephen told me when they were living with their dad and his girlfriend, the adults instructed the kids to hide when the police arrived. The kids already knew their designated spot, because their family viewed the "PoPo" not as protectors, but as the enemy.

In their first years with us, the kids had no direct contact with their birth families. Lynn started a Myspace account so we could share pictures with Brianna and Stephen's birth mom. We had also set up a post office box when she asked if she could mail something to the kids. She sent a ring and pair of earrings for Brianna and some old coins that had been her father's for Stephen. Even that upset Brianna, so we had to limit the birth mom's contact. We had no contact with their birth father.

Parker grieved the fact he didn't even know what his birth mom looked like. She had abandoned him to the state when he was three. He had no desire whatsoever to see his father again. In fact, the only emotion he showed toward him was fear. Parker's father, an abusive, scary man who ended up in jail on rape charges, lost his parental rights after a visit from which Parker returned to his foster parents' home with obvious signs of physical abuse.

Parker did have fond memories of his foster parents, and he grieved deeply that they chose not to adopt him. He thought he was part of their family all along. After all, he had lived with them multiple times during the seven years he spent in foster care. It surprised him to discover they had only taken him in the last time with the expectation that he would return home.

Years after we adopted Parker, I realized that much of his most trying behavior had to do with the goal of getting back to this foster family. At the age of four, he would go live with an aunt or another family member and end up right back with this foster family when things didn't work out. I think he figured if he behaved badly enough, we would give up on him and he could go back.

It was challenging to remember the kids were going through extreme grief and loss. I had hoped and even expected them to fully enter our family from the beginning, but that didn't allow them space to grieve and feel. Being taken from their birth families left a huge hole in their lives, regardless of how unsafe those families were.

The loss of my sister-in-law years later to cancer reminded me how those feelings of loss remain intense for a long time. Grieving is not an easy or quick process.

Getting Gas

As I picked the kids up from school the next week, Stephen greeted me with visible anger. My best guess was that he was mad that he had to walk all the way to the van — our normal pickup spot. The day before, I had met him at his classroom so I could talk to his teacher. Since Stephen struggled with unrealistic expectations, if I did something extra once, he expected me to do it from then on.

Brianna, who tended to be very social, came to the car more than fifteen minutes late. She did this often, despite being disciplined for it over and over again. She knew she was making everyone wait but didn't seem to care. She wanted to hang out with friends. Since we had waited on her so long, she gave energy back to the rest of us by doing an extra chore when we got home.

I stopped to get gas on the way home. I had barely turned toward the gas pump when my attention was diverted to three children pounding on the van windows like little, starving birds, chirping loudly for their mama to feed them. I smiled and waved. They waved back.

I turned around to put the credit card in, and they pounded, escalating each moment I wasn't looking directly at them. I forced a smile and waved off and on, trying to placate them. Toward the end, I opted to ignore the loud banging so I could actually pump gas.

After I finished getting gas, I turned around and dropped the nozzle, which seemed to have gotten much heavier than it was five minutes earlier, into its resting place. I could feel resentment building over their inability to handle even one second without my attention.

As I got back into the van, I realized I had forgotten to get milk and bread earlier that day. We really needed them, but the thought of walking into the store with the kids made me want to crawl into a hole and die.

Trips to the Store

My first trip to the grocery store with Brianna and Stephen proved disastrous. Little hands grabbed everything in sight, and little mouths loudly announced their presence. Seeing the judgmental stares and shaking of heads, I wanted to wear a sandwich board with arrows pointing to each child, next to the words, "I didn't cause this."

I struggled with feeling angry at those judging what they didn't understand. People assumed I was a bad mom without knowing these kids had been in my home only a couple of weeks. I also hated feeling so embarrassed. I wished I could stop worrying about what others thought of me.

After the first couple of trips to the store, I wised up and made the kids keep two hands on the cart at all times as we walked, or they would spin out of control as early as the produce aisle. When Parker came, I'm sure we looked funny with three children side-stepping as they walked alongside the cart.

Bri and Stephen caught on to the fact that sometimes I would surprise those who behaved well with a reward. After they proved they could handle walking with two hands on the cart, they could graduate to only having to put one hand on the cart. Once they did that well, they could simply walk beside the cart.

After experiencing small success after small success, trips to the store were less frequently walks down the hall of mommy shame.

Parker still made shopping trips miserable. I had to hold his hand. Otherwise he would run off, grab things, or do something else to create chaos. He constantly wiped his forehead, causing people to look at us funny. He talked loudly as soon as we entered the store. Most of the time he would wiggle his entire body as he walked beside me in a way that made him look like the wacky, waving tube man you see at used car dealerships.

I would look at pitying or critical onlookers, offer a frail smile, and hope no one would comment about his lack of eyelashes. We couldn't stop him from plucking them out when we weren't looking.

One time, tired of what seemed to be his determination to embarrass me, I said in a loud, silly voice, "Are you trying to embarrass me?" For some reason, he lost a little bit of his wiggle after that. Still, I would have much rather had a "shopper fairy" grace me with groceries instead of having to go into a store with Parker.

The People of Walmart

The most embarrassing moments came with the meltdowns. Sometimes we would turn right around and leave the store without being able to get what we needed. The first week of February, we could have had our picture taken for the People of Walmart website when Parker had the worst meltdown ever. We had shopped without incident, so I relaxed, thinking we were out of the woods.

As the cashier handed my credit card back to me, I grabbed Parker's hand and let out a sigh of relief to have made it.

"OK, guys, we're running late to get home so let's walk fast back to the car."

"I HAVE to go to the bathroom!"

"Parker, I feel like this is a game. You know we are running late. You can go to the bathroom as soon as we get home. It only takes ten minutes to get there."

"But I HAVE to go!"

"You'll have to wait, Bud." I tried to hurry him out of the store before he escalated, but as we passed the bathrooms, Parker threw himself on the ground, grabbed his crotch, and began doing a pee-pee dance of sorts on the floor, in full view of everyone leaving the store.

"I HAVE to PEE!" he kept shouting repeatedly.

"SHUT UP!" I whispered loudly, hoping to at least stop the yelling.

Until that point, I'd never spoken those words to any of my children, but in that moment they tumbled out of my mouth.

As he continued his meltdown, a scene flashed before my eyes.

So this is where it's going to happen. Here I've held it together all this time and this will be the moment I snap and beat the pulp out of him. It is going to be right here, in the middle of Walmart. Twenty people will have their phones out, recording my entire emotional breakdown, and then they'll call CPS.

Luckily, I got him out of the store. When we arrived home, Parker went about his afternoon routine as if nothing had happened.

"Parker, weren't you telling me at the store how badly you needed to go to the bathroom? Why haven't you even attempted to go into the bathroom yet?" I felt irritated that he had forgotten he had to go. Once again it seemed that he was purposefully manipulating me.

"Oh... yeah. That's right," he said quietly.

"Well, you made such a huge stink about it, you'd BETTER go now!"

I wish I'd known then that he wasn't trying to make our lives miserable.

Dancing with a Porcupine

When Parker was tested for autism, we discovered that when he experienced anxiety, his brain function shut down significantly. During those times, he became unable to process information, handle emotions, think, or remember. My attempt to hurry him likely triggered his anxiety.

YOU Didn't get the MILK!

As I drove home from the gas station, I noticed a dead squirrel on the side of the road and cringed. I hoped the kids hadn't seen it, but I heard Stephen yell, "Ah, sweet! Look at that!" as he pointed out the carcass.

I looked back and saw all three children's faces light up with glee, their eyes riveted toward the road kill.

"Awesome!"

"So cool!"

Their intense fascination with death and dead things made my stomach churn every time.

After arriving home, Stephen looked inside the fridge to get a snack. He turned to me, eyes shooting darts of rage, and hissed, "*YOU* didn't get *MILK*!" By the sound of his tone, you'd have thought I'd just murdered a litter of puppies.

The intensity of his comment felt like an arrow, aimed at letting me know I had failed him. It seemed like all three kids zealously searched for ways I had let them down so they could point out how I had completely failed them as a mom and couldn't be trusted.

I couldn't count the times one of them would ask a question to which they knew the answer would be "no," and then storm off when they got the expected answer. It was as if they were looking for a reason to be mad.

"You don't have to create a situation to justify being mad at me," I'd say to them. "It's OK if you don't know why you're mad."

Many of the kids' perceived offenses were so minor that if they hadn't happened continuously, I would have found humor in them. But it didn't matter how much I gave or how hard I tried to communicate that I loved them; the message I got back was always, "You don't love me. You can't take care of me."

As the other two ate their snack, Parker threw himself on the living room floor and began a three-year-old style tantrum because I wouldn't let him have candy.

From day one with us, this child obsessed over sweets. The move intensified his obsession. He would fish sugary items out of the trash can if I didn't stop him. It was as if sugar was easier to take in than love. This outburst only lasted fifteen minutes, and we eased into our afternoon routine.

Parker's latest tantrum hadn't lasted as long as it usually did, but the screaming got on my nerves and made it hard to remember that Parker wasn't in control of himself. Many times he seemed fully in control, so it was easy to forget that trauma shuts down certain parts of the brain.

I'd seen brain scans of a child who'd been through trauma compared to those of a typical child. The scan of the child who had been through trauma looked like Swiss cheese. Almost all of their brain activity occurs in the "fight-flight-or-freeze" part of the brain, with little activity in the cerebral cortex — the part of the brain that allows us to think and process rationally.

Still, Parker's actions caused constant internal conflict as I struggled to understand the difference between willful defiance and being genuinely unable to regulate his emotions.

CHAPTER 8

Look at My Artwork!

Parker stood in front of me, holding out his artwork so I could see. "Look, Mom! Look what I made!"

"Wow, Buddy! That is incredible! I love the colors you used and the details. You did such a good job… you should feel proud of yourself! Why don't you put it on the fridge?"

Evidently that wasn't enough. He continued to stand there, pushing the paper toward me as if he were poor Oliver Twist saying, "Please, sir, I want some more!"

"Good job, Bud!"

He continued to stand there, a goofy, expectant smile on his face.

"OK, Parker. I know you want more praise, but that's all I'm going to give right now. I'd like you to put it on the fridge."

Parker stood there for a moment longer, hoping I'd play cheerleader again, but I was already talking with Brianna about her day. After putting his creation on the fridge, Parker, who was jealous of any attention directed at someone besides him, tried to interrupt my conversation so loudly and persistently that I sent him to his room so Brianna could get a sentence out.

The more attention I gave the kids, the more they demanded from me, much like a starving person gulping food when they are finally able to eat.

Bri would go so far as to make herself hiccup for attention. Stephen made constant noise. Parker, if he had my undivided attention, would panic and start talking about nothing because he didn't want the attention to stop. We had to limit the time on his tales to prevent him from describing each little flower on a Super Mario video game or reciting every minute detail of a book he was reading.

It was as if I were a pizza and they needed to battle one another to make sure they got every piece and no one else got any. Earlier that week, I explained it even less appetizingly to my best friend, Becky.

"I feel like a piece of roadkill along the highway with three vultures picking the meat off my bones, asking, 'Is that all you've got?'"

Prader-Willi Syndrome

"It will NEVER be enough, no matter what you do," the kids' therapist told me at our next appointment.

She explained that when a child has gone through severe neglect, abuse, or trauma, their heart becomes like Swiss cheese, a bucket with holes in it, or even a bucket with no bottom at all. You can endlessly give, but the child still feels they need more. It didn't matter how much I gave or how hard I worked.

She went on to say that giving the kids too much attention in the beginning was probably not healthy for them. They needed to learn that healthy adults take care of themselves; their lives don't revolve solely around their children. They needed to know that a healthy family makes sure everyone's needs are met.

I had fed into their selfishness, keeping them from feeling emotions they needed to deal with. I thought I was doing what was best for them, but I had prevented them from growing as much as they could have.

Her words made me think of a middle schooler who attended youth group where I worked as a youth director in my late twenties. This young man had Prader-Willi Syndrome, a rare disorder that causes a body to signal insatiable hunger, even when the person has eaten plenty. This child's parents had to install locks on the cupboards and fridge to prevent him from killing himself by eating too much.

Much like the parents who had to ignore their son's desire for food, I couldn't always trust my children's cues about how much attention, praise, or time they needed. It was like an emotional version of Prader-Willi Syndrome – their minds always signaled the need for more attention and love, never feeling full or satisfied.

I had to learn to determine the difference between legitimate needs and wants.

I found this revelation freeing. However, though I understood that my kids' desire for attention was sometimes misplaced, it was difficult to ignore the constant requests for more.

I was working myself to death, trying to meet all of my kids' perceived needs. I needed to decide ahead of time how many games I would play or how long I would sit and talk, so I could maintain my own sanity while helping them learn healthy boundaries. I also had to remind myself that if I chose not to give them attention out of irritation, I was allowing their behavior to control me.

How to Go to the Bathroom

After getting home from work, Lynn stayed in the living room with the kids so I could finally go to the bathroom. I'd needed to go for at least an hour, but it was too much of a hassle when Lynn wasn't there.

As if the Pied Piper of Hamelin had drawn them with magical tunes, Brianna and Stephen followed me back into the hallway. They pretended to have a conversation with each other in the hall while I went to the bathroom, their voices raised to a volume and pitch that could have raised the dead. The message I got was that they were mad I was away from them, even for a moment. It was suffocating.

For crying out loud! Can't they entertain themselves for one minute while I go to the bathroom? It's not like I'm abandoning them!

When Lynn wasn't home, I had to send all three kids to their rooms and make sure the chimes were on to prevent Armageddon from occurring in the hallway outside the bathroom. I learned later that one reason Bri freaked out was that her mom did drugs in the bathroom and she was afraid I would, too.

I thought back to the first time I tried to take a ten-minute nap. I had taken the kids to the circus, and Lynn had given specific instructions to the kids about being quiet and letting me sleep.

Walking through the hallway, Stephen was as quiet as a ninja. But once directly in front of my room, he yelled as loudly as he could, "Hey, Brianna!"

At that moment I realized my own home was no longer a sanctuary.

Things hadn't changed much since then.

Lynn, familiar with this game, called the kids back into the living room. There they pretended to play, their amplified voices letting me know they were still out there, waiting for my attention.

I took a minute to sit in the bathroom and breathe. I knew the Pied Piper would soon call two children back into the hallway. There they would escalate to the point of hurting each other even with Lynn there, if I didn't come out soon enough for their liking.

I dragged myself out of the bathroom to finish dinner.

"Mom! Look at this!" Stephen yelled. I wasn't even in the kitchen yet, and Stephen was attached to my hip, trying to get in my face and have his hands all over my arms. As usual, I had to pry him off to simply breathe.

"Stephen, I love you and love being around you, but you need to stop getting in my face."

"Mom! Mom! Mom!" Brianna said, trying to get me to look at her instead of her brother.

I hugged them both. "OK, both of you need to find something to do because I need to finish making dinner."

"OK kids, come back into the living room," Lynn called. If he hadn't been home, I would've had to complete dinner with all the kids in my direct line of sight. Now they sat on either side of him, battling for his attention.

Will You Play a Game?

After dinner, we told the kids to pick up their dirty dishes. "Where do I put my plate?" Parker asked, knowing perfectly well where the dirty dishes went. "I'm sure you'll figure it out, my dear," I replied.

"But I don't know where to put it," he continued to say, getting louder each time.

My body tensed up, fearing another meltdown, but I said nothing. Seeing that the rest of us had already gone into the living room, he gave up and put the plate on the counter where it belonged.

Later, Parker came out from playing in his room into the living room where we were all hanging out.

"Will you play a game with me?" Parker asked Lynn and me.

"Parker, we've already answered that question. Not tonight," Lynn said. This was the tenth time he had asked over the past 30 minutes. I was getting tired of redirecting him. I knew from experience it wouldn't be the last time he would make this same request.

Five minutes later, he came out again. "Will you play a game with me?"

I clenched my teeth and prepared to give him a lecture.

"Parker, if you're asking me if I love you, the answer is yes," came my husband's reply.

I looked curiously over at Parker and watched to see how he would react. Neither of us had ever responded this way before, and I wanted to see what would happen.

"OK." Parker went off to play. He didn't ask again, and what felt like a mind game was over.

Parker was sending what I later learned to call a "miscued message." He outwardly communicated that he wanted us to interact with him every moment, but really, he simply needed constant reassurance of our love.

That realization helped keep us from getting frustrated over the constant demand for attention. After this, we more easily recognized his need and would simply say, "If you're asking if I love you, the answer is yes."

This wasn't the only way his "miscued messages" were communicated.

Parker's behaviors made it feel like he was working hard to pay me back for my absence. For years, it frustrated and angered me.

Finally, I realized he was trying to say, "I missed you." After that, when he acted out I'd say, "I missed you too, Buddy," and the acting out lessened considerably.

With all three kids, I had to constantly remind myself that the message I received wasn't always what they intended. What came out as "I hate you" was their way of saying, "I'm feeling insecure about your love for me right now.
I need to know you love me no matter what."

Misbehavior was their way of saying, "My feelings are hurt" or "I'm feeling scared." Many times they were really asking, "Do you love me? How about now? What about if I do this? Will this stop you from loving me?"

Come Pick Him Up

I had been in the house ten minutes when my cell phone rang.

Seeing the school system's exchange number come up on the screen, I felt my heart pound. The message would most likely not be good.

For the first two years, it was anyone's guess as to which child they were calling about, but by this time I knew they were calling about Parker.

"You have to come pick up Parker," the voice on the other end said. "He's completely out of control today."

This had become a common occurrence since the move. The teacher and administration felt compassion for me, so his behavior had to get bad before they called.

Only a week before, he had been kicked out of school for three days. I knew I couldn't handle having him home for that long, so we sent him to respite with Ann and Trent, a wonderful couple who occasionally watched the kids.

While Parker's classroom teacher had done a great job with him over the past year and a half, the move had caused him to regress.

With this latest call from the school, the closer I got to picking him up, the tighter the knot in my stomach grew. The next few hours would be a nightmare, and I would have little energy left for the other two after school.

As expected, I picked up a very angry Parker, who spent the afternoon melting down, wailing, asking questions he knew the answer to, and making cutting remarks.

That night, Parker turned to hug Lynn good night and walked right past me, sneering.

All of the kids knew how to deliver a well-placed punch through their comments or looks.

After the move, I heard "I hate you" more often than I cared to remember. Many of their ongoing behaviors communicated a similar sentiment. Sometimes the words were so cutting that Lynn would ask, "You guys wanna just take a knife and stab Mom in the back instead?"

"Why does he have to make it so obvious?" I would lament to Lynn, later.

"Don't take it so personally," Lynn reminded me, trying to help.

Each time Lynn said this, I wanted to punch him in the face. In the back of my mind, I knew the kids would have acted this way toward any mom who adopted them. I could have been June Cleaver and they still would have pushed me away.

I'd read quotes like the one by Dr. Karyn Purvis, author of *The Connected Child*, that says, "It is not you against this child. It is you and this child against this child's history. It's not a personal attack on you."

Sometimes knowing this didn't help. Sometimes the kids' sharp-as-a-knife jabs and behaviors aimed at keeping me at a distance still hurt. It felt personal, and it was hard to let the hurtful actions and words roll off my back.

It felt like my children were creating the waves of rejection, but they were being pulled under by those same waves. They weren't against me. They were victims, drowning in old wounds.

When I set out to help wounded children heal, I became a lifeguard treading deep waters of pain.

When I first experienced how children who have endured trauma try to push others away and control those around them, it made me mad.

Lynn had a more insightful take: "It's not really them trying to get control; it's more that they're drowning and trying to grab onto anything around them to keep themselves from going under."

In those times of treading deep waters with my children, I needed to hold on to something stable in order to help them. Lifeguards don't race into the water without a life preserver. Otherwise, they and the person they're trying to save would both drown.

It was time to look for help.

CHAPTER 9

Doctor Visit

By the time I went to the doctor, the stress of the move and the increased behaviors had taken a toll.

"If you don't get rid of your stressors, you're going to die."

As I drove home from the appointment, my anger toward God surfaced.

"Where are you? You're the one who told me to do this. Why have you abandoned me?"

The silence made me feel even more alone.

My life's verse had always been Romans 8:28: "And we know that in all things God works for the good of those who love Him, who have been called according to His purpose."

Over and over, I had watched God work in my life, even showing up miraculously in a healing from hypoglycemia, documented by a doctor, and later, much-needed emotional healing. I had watched Him take challenging situations and bring beauty from the ashes time and time again when I got to the other side.

I don't see how this is going to work for my good. Maybe I need a new verse.

I came home, struggling to figure out what to do. Despite my fatigue, I forced myself to prepare dinner that night.

Almost as soon as I began, Stephen paced, stomping up and down on the dining room floor, pounding on the walls, kitchen counters, and table. Dinner prep was a hard time for all the kids.

"Bloop, plap, flap, bloopedy-boop, glop, glap, flibity, plop," Stephen added nonsense noise into the mix, getting louder and louder until he got the attention he desired.

"Stephen, it seems like you really like to make noise. I'd like you to sit on this bar stool and make noise for me."

At times, Lynn and I would require the kids to "practice" a behavior we didn't want them to do. We used the excuse that if they were going to do something, they may as well be good at it.

The real reason we did it was that, for the most part, if the kids knew it didn't bother us, making them practice the behavior took away their motivation to keep doing it. Sometimes, requiring Stephen to make noise or talk for a prescribed amount of time caused him to stop, at least for a while.

"But I don't want to."

"I know, but I'd like you to, so come over and make some noise for me for five minutes."

He pulled himself onto the bar stool. Though he had been able to make plenty of noise a few minutes earlier, he struggled to do so. Eventually, he managed to squeak out a bit of noise for me.

My Little Hypochondriac

Not only was Stephen quite the noisemaker, he was also a hypochondriac. Daily he'd bring me at least one imaginary ailment, yet if he injured himself, he never said a word about it.

At first it didn't bother me when Stephen used one boo-boo or another to get extra attention from me. But after the move, it intensified to the point that it became annoying.

"What do I do?" I asked the therapist. "He is driving me crazy with one injury after another, all aimed at getting my constant attention."

"Kiss every boo-boo as if he were dying. Be over dramatic, yet not sarcastic."

She hoped the dramatics would fill whatever need he seemed to have and lessen his need for more attention.

I tried her method, though I found it hard not to be sarcastic. Despite the dramatics, Stephen's antics continued — lessening, but never going away.

Her second plan worked brilliantly. The next time he faked an illness, I was walking him to the car after school. He listed at least five big boo-boos by the time we reached the car.

"Sweetheart, I'm really concerned about you. Your poor body is falling apart. When we get home, I would like you to go to bed and stay there so we can make sure your body has time to heal."

"Oh... no, that's OK. I'm feeling fine."

"We need to make sure your body gets rest so it has a chance to heal. I want to make sure you're being taken care of."

For the rest of that day and the next, I made him stay in bed and rest. I gave him chicken noodle soup and pampered him like he was sick, but didn't let him leave the bed, because "his poor body needed to heal." It was the last time he complained about non-existent aches and pains.

Queenhood

As I worked on dinner, Parker went back to play in his room, and the only reason Brianna wasn't by my side was because she sat on the couch, eyes glued to the driveway. "DAD's home!" Bri shouted.

Bri had recently started to wait at the window for at least thirty minutes before Lynn came home so she could be the first one to notice he had arrived. It was as if noticing him first made her closer to him than the rest of the family. As soon as he walked in the door, she attempted to monopolize his attention.

The summer before our move, Bri began squeezing herself between Lynn and me as we walked together, then moving over as if to push me out. I found it odd. As these behaviors became more frequent and overt, I mentioned them to the therapist.

Later, in a therapy session, Bri would talk about wanting to kill me so she could have Lynn to herself. With that said, divorce seemed to be her preferred method of taking me out of the picture. Purposefully sweet to him and mean to me, she worked a plan to build a wedge between Lynn and me. Sometimes she was successful.

Brianna pitted herself in competition against me. If I petted the dog, she would try to call the dog over so she could pet him instead. It was as though I was constantly vying for "Queenhood" of the family. She worked to dethrone me at every opportunity. If I left for even a short time, she'd attempt to assume the role of being in charge. Brianna's main goal was to be more important to Lynn than anyone else was, especially me.

The week before, she told me, "I want to replace you."

Confused, I asked for clarification. "What do you mean by that?"

"I want to be more important to Dad than you are."

She started to lie, claiming that Lynn had told her things he hadn't said, in an effort to demonstrate that he was sharing more with her than with me. Silly things, mostly.

"Oh, by the way, *DAD* told me it's supposed to be cold today," she'd say, emphasizing his title in such a way that indicated they had a closer relationship than Lynn and I did.

"Did you tell Brianna it was going to be cold today?" I'd ask, more out of curiosity than anything.

"No," he'd say, looking at me strangely. "I didn't even get a chance to talk to her this morning."

Brianna became insanely jealous when Lynn did things for me. She was particularly jealous that he had changed the ring tone on my phone to an old car horn when he called.

"Whenever you hear that horn, picture me ogling you," he said to me with a wink.

After that, she frequently tried to steal my phone and change the ring tone.

Death Glares

Lynn walked in, and all the kids ran toward him. After giving them hugs and hearing a little bit about their day, he met me in the kitchen and gave me a hug.

After his big hug for me, he asked, "So how was your appointment? What did the doctor..."

"Blurp, blab, dub-e-dub, hip, blab, blip," Stephen started to make loud nonsense noises once again. None of the kids liked it when Lynn and I interacted.

"Stephen, stop it," Brianna said in her usually bossy way. Then, she stepped over to stand between Lynn and me as if she had been invited into our conversation. Before we could correct her, Parker had chimed in.

"Mom, can I watch TV?"

The kids NEVER watched TV on a school night except for a half hour starting at 8:00, and it was only 6:00 pm.

"Parker, you've lived in this house long enough to already know the answer," I said. Then I announced, "OK, since Dad and I need to talk and you guys are not making healthy choices, I'd like you all to hang out in your rooms until we have finished talking."

I heard noise coming from the family room. Parker had turned on the TV.

"Parker, what a bummer! After Dad and I talk, you can fill the dishwasher to give back energy."

I knew it was way more likely he was going to drain my energy than to give any back, but it was the only consequence I could think of at the time.

"What? You said I could watch it!"

"Sweetheart, you know I didn't. Turn the TV off."

He pretended not to hear me.

I turned toward Parker. "Thank you so much for letting me know you're too tired to listen. Since I'm such a good mom, I'm going to have you go to bed early so you can get rested up." I tried to keep things lighthearted, but inwardly I was fuming.

Mercifully, we were past the point where every little instruction elicited a WWIII-intensity argument. This time, as I turned off the TV, he simply shot me what could only be described as a "death glare" and went to his room.

I made a mental note, knowing I'd need to ensure before bedtime the chime on his door was working and my bedroom door was locked. When I had received a particularly high number of death glares in a day, I pictured waking up to him standing over me with a knife.

We kept the dog in our room so Parker couldn't hurt him in the middle of the night. Only a few months earlier, his school staff had sat us down to warn us: "We can't formally diagnose Parker at such a young age, but if he were 18, he would be labeled a sociopath."

Lynn and I nodded our heads in agreement. At the time, it made sense, but inwardly I was freaking out. That word made his alarming behavior more real and scary.

The next time I took him to therapy, I talked to the kids' therapist about it.

"Of course he would be labeled a sociopath."

I spit out the water I was about to swallow. I'd expected her to debunk their words. "WHAT? What do you mean by that? Are you sure?"

"Yes, I'm sure."

She looked over and offered what I could only imagine was meant to be a reassuring smile. I didn't feel reassured.

"Keep in mind he's young. There's plenty of time to help him heal."

Despite our precautions and what others had told us, Lynn thought my fear of being killed was crazy. After all, Parker didn't give death glares when Lynn was around.

The Only Way to Have a Conversation

I hated that we had to send the kids to their rooms, but at this point it was the only way to carry on an uninterrupted conversation.

It amazed me how the children couldn't seem to hear what we told them from two feet away but could hear an entire, whispered conversation from the other side of the house. For a long time, private conversations took so much extra work that we gave up. Intimate conversations became almost nonexistent.

One Saturday afternoon, Lynn and I needed to talk through some logistical issues regarding the kids. Rather than send them to their rooms, we went to ours. Sitting them down in the living room, Lynn issued instructions: "Mom and I are going to talk in our room for just a few minutes. Do not knock on our door unless there's a fire or blood."

Later, when I understood more about my kids' thought processes, I realized that we had basically given them a challenge. We may as well have said, "Let's see who can start a fire first!"

About one and a half minutes into our conversation, there was a rap, rap, rap at the door.

"Is someone bleeding?" Lynn inquired.

"No."

"Is there a fire?"

"No."

"Then why are you knocking on this door?"

"We broke your computer," they replied in unison.

I knew there was an ever-so-slight possibility it had been an accident, but deep in my heart I believed they broke it on purpose. I never got a complete picture of what happened, but from the ungodly amount of noise I had heard from the living room moments before, I imagine they were wrestling right next to it and somehow guided their "play" toward Lynn's work laptop and broke the screen.

We had inadvertently done an experiment and discovered that in less than two minutes, all hell would break loose if we weren't within eyesight. Two minutes isn't a long time.

We made the kids work off the cost of the repairs, but our little experiment cost more than $600.

What Did the Doctor Say?

Once the kids were in their rooms, Lynn turned to me. "What did the doctor say?"

"She said I was going to die if I didn't get rid of my stressors."

"What? What did she mean by that?"

"I don't know. I didn't even think to ask because I was too shocked. As far as getting rid of my stressors, we both know it would be impossible. Although earlier I was thinking having three square meals a day alone in prison sounded pretty inviting."

We both chuckled. At least we hadn't lost our sense of humor, though it had darkened over the past two years. We were often shocked at the things we had to laugh at to remain sane.

"What else did she say?"

"She was pretty concerned about me not getting sleep, so she gave me something to help with it. She also gave me some supplements. Oh, and she told me to rest while I ate... like THAT is ever going to happen! I'm lucky if I even eat most days!"

"How was *your* day?"

"It was OK. Get this — I was talking with one of my co-workers, and she asked how we were doing. I told her, 'We are SO tired.' Do you know what she said?"

"What?"

"She said, 'Yeah, three kids will do that.'"

"Seriously?"

"Yeah. People who haven't done this have no idea what it's like."

After we finished talking, we called for the kids. Bri came out, asking, "So, what did you guys talk about?" as if being privy to our conversations was her God-given right.

"It was a little bit of None-Yo!" my husband said with a sly smile, referring to our silly abbreviation of "none of your business" that came from having to say it so frequently.

She worked so hard to invade our relationship that we even purchased a white-noise machine to put between our rooms so she couldn't listen to our conversations or other activities at night in our bedroom.

As Brianna huffed off to the corner of the living room, Stephen resumed with the chatter and nonsense noise.

"Aha, uhu, uhu, uhu, bup, blap, roopen-flappen, blip, sap, sop, boop, blap"

"Stephen, why don't you come and sit with me. You need to stop with the noise," Lynn said as he walked to the living room.

Sanitized Stories

Thankfully, dinner was almost ready. I walked into the living room.

"Stephen, I'd like you to set the table." It was his turn.

"Me?"

Lynn chortled. "How many other Stephens are there?"

"But I don't know how to set the table."

He'd been setting the table for more than two years.

I put my hand on his shoulder. "I'm sure you'll figure it out. You're a smart boy."

As I added the finishing touches to dinner, I looked over to see Stephen scattering the silverware, plates and cups all over the table. "It's obvious you're mad about something. What's going on?"

I glanced over just in time to catch Lynn, who was getting himself a drink, give his "not this again" look. I may have even noticed a slight eye roll. He believed I played therapist way too often with the kids and that I saw anger where there was none.

Stephen stopped tossing silverware and looked at me. "I'm mad you were gone the other day."

Hoping to just get dinner on the table, I said, "I'm sure it was tough for you and it brought up all sorts of feelings for you, Stephen. I know it sometimes makes you feel abandoned, but I love you, and I'm not going to leave you."

After a long pause, I added, "*NOW* do you know how to set the table?"

"Yes." Miraculously, his memory returned as he moved the dinnerware to the correct spots.

I looked over to see a slight look of shock on Lynn's face.

The "other day" he was referring to had been almost two weeks before, when I played Bunco while Lynn stayed home with the kids. This monthly game was about the only thing I did outside the home.

My sister-in-law, Lisa, had invited me to play with the group when Brianna and Stephen first moved in with us. Each month, the ladies asked me how things were going, showing genuine concern for me and my family. I knew they prayed for us on a regular basis, and they didn't seem to mind that for a long time my answers showed little progress. I loved their hearts, and I left feeling more energized.

Despite their love and concern, I also left Bunco feeling increasingly isolated. Throughout the night as women gabbed about getting their nails done or what color they were going to paint their living room, I simply smiled and nodded.

We'd spent so much money replacing things like cell phones that we didn't have money for manicures, and just the thought of another home project made me want to die from exhaustion.

As the conversations steered toward how well their children were doing in sports, I mentally reviewed our last therapy session, where one of the kids revealed atrocious abuse endured at the hand of a drunken adult.

I felt like a freak, shouldering the pain of the world. My life centered around topics people didn't talk about at parties, and I didn't want to share things that would embarrass my kids. I lived in a world no one wanted to visit, where bad things happened to little children and ugly behavior overtook all joy and laughter.

I learned early on that most people could not handle the intensity of my emotions or knowing what I was really going through, so I softened things as I spoke. How do you share feeling tortured, hopeless, and in despair when someone asks in passing, "How are you?"

I developed a love-hate relationship with the question. Should I go superficial, pasting a fake smile on my face and offering up a quick, "fine," then hurrying off before they could see the tears forming? Or brace myself for the glazed-over look I'd inevitably meet when I shared just the tip of the iceberg?

At times, I wasn't even honest with myself.

Had I been honest, I don't even know if words could adequately describe what I felt. Raw. Vulnerable. Grieving. Wounded. Lifeless.

How do you describe the pain of watching three children make damaging choices that could affect them forever? Or the anger I felt at those who had hurt them and the system that had failed them? Or feeling beaten down by my kids' anger and lashing out?

Years later, I read a blog post by Sarah Bessey called "Sanitized Stories We Tell." She summed up how I felt interacting with most people: "It makes me wonder how much pressure we feel to sanitize our stories so that they don't make people uncomfortable, how we anecdote our experience with the lightness or the healing or birth or new life alone in order to make it acceptable. We simplify and sanitize and so we miss the healing we could have if we only spoke the whole truth."

CHAPTER 10

Shower and Bedtime

As bedtime neared, Lynn walked over to Parker. "I'd like you to go take your shower."

"In which bathroom?"

We had only one working bathroom at the time.

"I'll let you figure that one out on your own."

"But I don't know!" Parker wailed.

"You're smart. You'll figure it out."

After we ignored his pleas for help, Parker finally managed to find his way and, in theory, took a shower.

It was rare that Parker actually washed his hair and body in the shower, so I was usually the unfortunate soul who had to do the "sniff test" afterwards. Having sniffed a definitely-not-washed head of hair, it was obvious Parker's body had not been touched by any soap-like substance, although his hair was wet.

"Go back and try again."

"But I really washed!" he howled.

My body tensed. I didn't even realize I had stopped breathing.

"Parker, go back and wash NOW."

He pulled himself together and went back into the bathroom. Water ran, but again no soap was used.

One more sniff test. One more insistence of having washed.

Relieved because it only took two times to produce the smell of shampoo, I didn't even worry about smelling his arm. I was tired. I just needed him to go to bed.

I walked into my room, tempted to climb into bed right away. I moved my tongue around my mouth and felt fuzzy sweaters developing on the front of my teeth.

My entire life, I'd had a night-time routine of changing into pajamas, brushing my teeth, and washing my face and moisturizing. Now it was all I could do to change into my pajamas. Sometimes I didn't even do that, as I let my exhausted body fall into bed fully clothed.

Remembering the doctor's advice, I figured I should reconsider and quickly brushed my teeth. *I'm so tired, but if I can just change into pajamas I'll be doing well*, I reassured myself as I slipped my legs into the soft fabric of my pajamas.

The Next Day

The next day I didn't wake up feeling much different, but I did notice I'd slept a little better than I had in a long time. I'd only gotten up six times that night, instead of the usual eight.

"I bet it's because of those meds she prescribed," I told Lynn that morning on the phone. He'd taken the kids to school on his way to work, allowing me to sleep in once again.

Lynn had been getting up with the kids on school mornings ever since the previous autumn, when I was homeschooling Brianna and Stephen. Since he knew how much energy homeschooling demanded of me, he felt it was only fair, especially since I was dealing with Parker's troublesome behaviors after school.

I felt a warmth towards him, knowing what a big deal it was. Parker was not a fun kid to deal with in the mornings. You could almost tell what kind of day it was going to be based on how he was dressed when he came out of the room. If any of his clothes were on backwards or inside out, or any buttons were askew, it was going to be a doozy. It was like an early-warning system for knowing how hellish the day would be.

Dancing with a Porcupine

Even with Lynn getting the kids ready in the morning, getting out of bed was a chore for me.

"The doctor is having me take Seriphos, which is supposed to lower my cortisol at night. She thinks mine is too high and that's why I'm not sleeping."

Everything I knew about cortisol came from weight-loss commercials. They called it the stress hormone, talking about how it made belly fat impossible to get rid of and announcing that their pill could overcome its effects.

It makes sense mine is high. I'd never weighed more in my entire life.

"Whatever the reason, I'm sure it feels good to sleep a little better," Lynn said.

"It's amazing how much sleep can affect everything." I still felt fatigued, but I was a little more energized for the day ahead.

I swallowed the handful of vitamins the doctor told me to take and sat down to eat. I had the quiet house to myself, except for Captain, who lay sleeping in the room near me. I thought the doctor's admonition not to do anything else while I ate was odd, but I figured I'd give it a go.

It felt weird to relax. Ever since the kids moved in I had become accustomed to being on high alert, waiting for the next shoe to drop. At the very least, I expected to get a call from the school any minute. *I don't think I can take one more day of him being home.*

Sitting down for breakfast for the first time in a long while, I heard the doctor's statement, "If you don't get rid of your stressors..."

I CAN'T get rid of my stressors. The thought kept circling back in my mind.

As I tried to figure out what changes to make, I thought about some of the stress in my life that had nothing to do with the kids. Despite feeling that God had asked me to step back from Forever Homes, I'd kept trudging along.

In addition to meeting with struggling moms, we were planning a benefit concert.

I need to stop trying to help so many people and help myself. I'm drowning while trying to save others.

I thought back to the conversation I'd had with Lynn the month before. Fearing what Lynn would say if I told him again that I needed to stop working for Forever Homes, I put the thought out of my mind. I felt resentment toward Lynn rising as I brainstormed ways to reduce my stress load.

Fake Tantrum

I looked at the clock and realized I would have to pick the kids up soon. I switched gears and racked my brain about how I could change my situation.

Aside from running away, which was tempting, I saw nothing I could change. My kids had come a long way, but their behaviors were still extreme. I couldn't wait for them to change before I reduced my stress level. At the current rate, I would die first.

Searching the Internet for books to help me, I chuckled at the title of a book called *Living Successfully with Screwed Up People*, by Elizabeth Brown. The name was funny, but the description made it seem the only book to fit the situation.

We are all screwed up right now. I clicked the mouse to purchase it and left to pick up the kids.

That afternoon, Parker threw a fit when I wouldn't let him have candy as an after-school snack.

He threw himself on the living room floor, screaming at the top of his lungs, flailing his arms and legs. I wondered how long this meltdown would last. Yesterday it was only fifteen minutes. The week before, we endured one forty-minute fit and another lasting several hours. That one had been in his room and included him throwing things at the wall and kicking the door.

I started to walk out of the room to get snacks for the other two, but watching him thrash around on the floor, I decided to take another approach.

I had read that if you surprise an out-of-control child, it may jar them from the "fight, flight or freeze" part of the brain back into the thinking part of the brain. Sometimes I would have the kids jump on the trampoline for the same effect, but when Parker was this far out of control, there was no way to get him out to the trampoline. I looked at Bri and Stephen, who stood to the side of the room, looking like war-torn veterans, and figured I'd give it a try.

Here goes nothing, I thought, as I flung myself on the ground and threw the biggest fake tantrum of my life. I acted my heart out, kicking and flailing my arms around, yelling at the top of my lungs.

Parker startled. "What the...?"

Brianna and Stephen giggled, looking at me like I'd lost my mind. Parker sat up and looked at me as if I'd grown antennas on top of my head. I stopped my tantrum and jumped to my feet.

"OK, kids, let's get going on our snack." I walked into the kitchen and patted the fuzz and dirt off my jeans from a carpet that hadn't seen a vacuum in a long time. Cleaning my house was the last thing on my mind.

Brianna and Stephen, still laughing and looking at each other like they had the craziest mother alive, followed me into the kitchen.

"Mom, I can't believe you just did that!" Brianna whispered, giggling.

"Hey, Mom! Remember when I was acting like a bird and you spit food in my mouth?" Stephen said. "That totally reminded me of when you did that!"

I winked at them and looked over in shock to see Parker calmly following us into the kitchen.

As the kids ate their snacks, I felt a wave of exhaustion flood over me. I thought about how hard I worked in the beginning to have fun with the kids. I tried to keep them on their toes as much as possible. They never knew what to expect from me. It saddened me that the stress of our situation had taken such a toll on my energy level that I wasn't able to be the fun mom anymore.

While the other two did homework, I pulled Parker into my lap.

"What's going on, Bud? You've been acting really angry lately."

"I hate you."

"Yeah, what else is going on?"

"I really hate you."

"You've already said that."

"I'm mad because I ruined my chances to play Wii for the week."

"I'm sure that's tough, Buddy. I can understand being upset about that. Is there anything else going on?"

"I'm mad you haven't given me enough attention."

"Parker, you keep going back to angry. You can sit here and continue to give me fluff or you can start being real and deal with what is going on. What's behind the anger, Bud? What emotion is the anger covering up? Hurt? Sadness? Fear?"

Parker looked down. "Fear."

"What are you afraid of?"

Parker looked up at me, his brown eyes tearing up. "I'm afraid that if I let myself not be angry, you will find out the things that happened to me. Then I'll lose another family, and no one else will want me."

I gave him a big hug. "Oh, Parker. No matter what you've been through, you'll always be part of our family. You don't have to worry about us giving up on you."

Tea Time

The following week, Parker was having a good day, and I was thankful for the brief reprieve from his tantrums. He'd been playing Legos in his room and came out while I made dinner.

"Hey, Mom. You know what we haven't done in a long time and what I really miss? TEA TIME!"

The first time we did Tea Time, I met the kids at the door after school, dressed in a large hat and an old, gaudy dress from our dress-up bin.

"All right, my dears," I'd said, in the best English accent I could muster. "It's time for tea."

The kids giggled.

"But before you join me for tea, you MUST dress up in an outfit."

"Aw, man!" they protested.

"No outfit, no tea. Aaaaaaand... you must speak with an accent."

I got more protests and eye rolls, followed by giggles as the kids ran to sift through the dress-up chest to find their outfit.

Despite my encouragement to expand their horizons, Bri and Stephen would choose the least creative outfits. Stephen walked into the dining room wearing a poncho Lynn had purchased while leading a mission trip to Ecuador before we were married. Bri wore a bright-blue Kimono robe I had purchased while on a month-long mission trip to Korea and Hawaii in high school. Parker wore the Mario costume he had worn for Halloween that year, as he used any excuse to wear the costume that mirrored his current video game obsession.

When the kids joined me, we ate snacks and finger foods and drank tea out of teacups from Goodwill. Requiring everyone to speak with an accent meant Tea Time involved lots of belly laughs.

Stephen, my little ham, had no qualms about trying out various accents, often mixing them together. Bri spent most of the time giggling to avoid speaking.

It became such a memorable time for them that for Christmas, Parker gave me a set of four tiny teacups from Starbucks, which he bought with money we gave him for shopping. We had often used these cups for Tea Time.

Although Tea Time had been one of our favorite activities, Parker may as well have asked me to run a marathon. "Oh, honey, I would love to, but I don't have the energy for that."

"Oh, OK." His shoulders slumped as he walked back into his room. I wanted to comfort him, but I didn't have the energy.

I thought back to Tea Time and all the other fun things I used to do with the kids after school. I would have loved to continue doing fun things — as well as "mom time" — like I had in our old house.

I still pulled them into my lap to ask about their day, but since the move I mostly did that when they needed to talk through issues.

These days I was just trying to survive.

After-School Swimming

I didn't have the emotional energy to orchestrate another Tea Time, but I did decide to start doing something with the kids after school again.

Despite my exhaustion, I signed our family up for a fitness center membership closer to home, so I could take the kids swimming. I reasoned that exercise would be good for me, and the kids could stand to blow off extra steam after school. Besides, I had started taking the vitamins the naturopath had recommended and was sure I'd feel better soon.

I tried to take the kids a few times each week, depending on how they were doing emotionally.

I could usually get at least a few laps in while Parker and Stephen attempted to get near-constant attention. They would go off to play for short intervals before coming back to my side.

Bri sometimes joined them, but unless I forced her to stay right by me, she went from person to person trying to get attention from women she found in the pool area. It wasn't good for her, but at times I just didn't have the energy to put a stop to it.

I kept a close eye on the kids as they played, because they needed intense supervision to be safe with each other. Sometimes, I decided it was time for a break and dropped them off at the kids' area while I walked on the treadmill.

The kids' area had video games powered by bicycles. Since Parker loved video games, he behaved well there. I found that the exercise counteracted the increased behavioral problems he typically displayed after playing video games.

As I slowly swam laps in the pool one day, I watched the kids playing and thought about how my decline in health had affected my parenting.

Those days, the thought of pulling them into my lap for a bowl of ice cream for mom time made my skin crawl. Instead of doing an art project with them, I set it up and watched or made dinner as they worked alone.

I also spent much more time insisting they find something to do, both because I wanted them to learn the important skill of self-entertaining and because I'd grown tired of having to interact with them every moment of their waking hours.

I used to write "I love you" notes with big smiley faces on the napkin in their lunches like my mom did when I was growing up, or leave notes or a surprise treat on their beds. Those became a rarity after the move.

What Can I Control?

Living Successfully with Screwed-Up People, the book I'd ordered, had finally arrived. With the exception of the days the school called and I picked Parker up early, I read it while the kids were at school. I didn't have a lot of energy, but I found reading helped my attitude.

I connected with the author's discussion about detachment. It seemed strange that to love my children better I needed to care less, but she was talking about a different kind of caring, one that didn't destroy me in the process.

Elizabeth Brown said:

> To stop the longing for what does not exist in screwed-up relation-
> ships, or to heal relationships that are beginning to skew, one must
> untangle from the emotions that swirl around or off a particular
> relationship. That process is called detachment. It basically means
> that you separate emotionally from the person around which your
> emotions swirl, in order to work on yourself, live your own life, feel
> your own feelings, and solve your own problems...Detachment is
> allowing others to be who they are, rather than who you believe
> they should be.

I was so focused on trying to change my kids that I entirely stopped working on my own life. I got so busy fixing their problems that I wasn't even aware of my own.

For me to survive, I had to let go of trying to make their lives turn out perfectly.

The need to let go was both frustrating and freeing. I wanted my children to do well. Sometimes I worked so hard to force them to make good choices that I damaged my relationship with them, creating more frustration within myself. In the end, my children were responsible for the choices they made. They had to decide how they wanted their lives to look and choose to move that direction.

Letting go of control was hard because I had to allow my children to fail much more than I had previously been willing.

As I improved at holding them accountable for their choices, my resentment decreased. Feeling angry toward my kids was an indication that I was working harder on a problem than they were. When I backed off, I could more easily look at their mistakes as learning opportunities rather than failures. My children got the message that they were capable of handling their lives, rather than feeling that they couldn't do life without me.

In Elizabeth Brown's book, she quoted a book I'd read years before, Melody Beattie's *Codependent No More*. "Sometimes detachment even motivates and frees people around us to begin to solve their problems. We stop worrying about them, and they pick up the slack and start worrying about themselves."

After reading that, I went back to my copy of *Codependent No More* and found a quote I previously underlined that read, "Detaching does not mean we don't care. It means we learn to love, care, and be involved without going crazy..."

Melody described what she saw when working with those living with alcoholics: "I saw people who had gotten so absorbed in other people's problems they didn't have time to identify or solve their own. These were people who had cared so deeply – and often destructively – about other people that they had forgotten how to care about themselves."

She was describing me.

Elizabeth Brown wrote that part of detaching was simply accepting your reality. That hit me. I was not accepting my reality. I was trying to force it to fit my dreams, and that wasn't working. I wasn't happy, and the kids weren't happy with me trying to fix them all the time. I wanted to be happy despite my difficult situation, and I was determined to figure out how.

CHAPTER 11

We Can No Longer Handle Him

By the end of March, I'd lost count of how many times I had to pick Parker up from school. His behaviors continued to escalate, so the school set up a special meeting with us.

"We can no longer handle him in the regular classroom," the principal started. "We've tried everything we can to help him here, but we can't do this anymore. He's making loud noises during class, constantly interrupting the teacher's instruction, and refusing to cooperate in class. If the teacher is working on language arts, he's working on the math that he refused to do earlier and then trying to force her to work with him on that instead. It's like he's trying to control her every move. He's running out of the classroom and hiding under tables and chairs. He is causing chaos in the five surrounding classrooms as well, so he's not just affecting his own classroom anymore."

"He pretty much freaked out when we moved," my husband said. "I'm so sorry you guys have had to deal with this. We knew what we were getting into and we CHOSE this. You didn't. We appreciate the hard work you have put into trying to help Parker be successful."

I sat there, wishing I would wake up to find this was all a big nightmare.

What are they going to do? I can't homeschool him!

"Thank you. Yes, well, we understand why his behavior has escalated, but we aren't equipped to handle him anymore."

Parker's teacher had worked so hard with him, but I could see how worn out she looked.

I gave her a weak smile. I appreciated her and felt sorry for all Parker had put her through over the past few months.

"What does this mean for him?" I asked the principal tentatively, afraid to hear the answer.

"We've arranged a couple hours of one-on-one tutoring at the library and a few hours in a special ed classroom geared toward children with severe behaviors."

"Please tell me it won't be the same teacher he had before." My heart was pounding through my chest.

"No. It's a smaller classroom, eight kids at the most, with a special ed teacher and one helper."

"What about the hours in between? There are a few hours unaccounted for in this scenario."

Please say there's something more.

"I'm afraid he will have to be home during the time in between. We don't have anything else to offer him," she said, looking down at the paper in front of her.

I felt my world fall apart. I was barely making it and could feel myself being pushed over the edge. I looked over at Lynn, hoping he had some magical words to say that would give us more services, but he didn't.

"Well, we appreciate that you've got something to offer him," he said. I didn't have the energy to speak.

The principal looked over at me. "I wish it was more."

I forced a smile and looked away, trying to hold back the tears.

I stood. The teacher walked over to me. We hugged, and I thanked her for all she had done for Parker. I knew she had gone above and beyond to try to help. I also knew she was struggling and burned out, just like I was, which gave me a sense of connection with her.

Dancing with a Porcupine

New Routine

The following week, we began our new routine. I'd barely get Parker off to the tutor before he returned for a few hours. I got a short break while he spent time in the behavioral classroom until I had to pick him up after school.

On the first afternoon, I felt the knot in the pit of my stomach growing. I had to pick him up, and I'd seen him only a couple of hours earlier. When I drove up to the school, I saw the teacher, assistant and students from the behavioral class outside. The other kids were playing football. Parker was walking around the schoolyard alone, examining the grass as if he were looking for something.

The teacher saw me watching Parker with curiosity. "He's been trying to collect rocks during recesses. I'm Mrs. Pratt, Parker's teacher."

I introduced myself as Parker's mom. As we talked, Parker looked up from the grass and noticed I was talking to Mrs. Pratt. He ran toward me. Dramatically lifting his arms, he excitedly yelled "Mommy!" He jumped onto me and flung his arms around my neck, as if we'd been separated for years and he was thrilled to see his long-lost, beloved mother. I stood there motionless, my arms still by my side, stunned.

I was about to roll my eyes but realized his teacher was watching me. Afraid of being judged by this special ed teacher as I had been by the last, I figured I should try to look like the sweet, devoted mother I was, even though I knew his display of affection was for her sake. I forced a smile and tentatively patted his back, looking over at her nervously. Mrs. Pratt looked back and winked, letting me know that she understood his theatrical performance had been for her benefit.

Maybe she actually gets it.

I let out a sigh of relief and scraped Parker off me and set his feet on the ground. He looked over at her and batted his eyelashes. I looked at her face and could tell she wasn't buying his act. It felt good to finally have someone who understood. I'd become so tired of being misjudged.

Little did I know at this time how much of an impact Mrs. Pratt would make in Parker's life.

Warm, Fuzzy Love?

Three days later, Parker was stuck. As the bus dropped him off from tutoring, I could see it in his face. I also looked down and noticed his shirt was inside out. I knew it would be a tough afternoon, and I was in no mood to deal with his button-pushing. After he'd only been home for about ten minutes, I could no longer handle him badgering me with what felt like cruel mind games.

"Parker, you're going to have to do some work outside today."

"Why? Why should I have to do chores?"

"Well, Parker, you're not able to be in school full-time right now because of your choices. If you don't want to go to school, I will still love you. But, being the amazing mom that I am, it's my job to prepare you for life. Children who can't be in school need to learn how to do manual labor because those are usually the only jobs available to them."

I didn't tell him I'd picked an outside chore because I couldn't handle having him in the house just then. I could barely look at him. I was still too frustrated that I had to deal with his antics throughout the day because he was so out of control. Besides, it was April, and the weather was warm enough for him to wear shorts.

"That's not fair!"

"I'm sure this is tough for you, Parker, but you're going to have to do chores while you're at home until you decide school is important and can be there all day."

Parker followed me around trying to pull me into an argument, but after ten minutes of a one-sided argument, he got frustrated. He threw himself on the ground and wailed.

I can't take any more of this. I am going to hurt him if he doesn't stop.

I tried to drown out the wailing and attempted to get something done while he was screaming on the floor. It was hard to concentrate on anything.

After a half hour of non-stop wailing, Parker settled down and tried to argue with me again. I ignored him and offered him lunch, since it was about lunch time anyway. After he ate, I walked outside with him. I gave him instructions and came inside without him. He kept coming in, asking questions to which I was certain he knew the answer.

"But I don't know how to pull weeds."

"I already showed you how, Buddy," I said, shooing him outside.

Five minutes later, he came back in. "Did you want me to pull out all of the weeds?"

"You already know the answer to that, Parker. Go back outside."

After two more questions, I looked down and realized my body had begun to shake.

Out of desperation, I locked the door behind him. Parker pounded on the front door and screamed, demanding I let him in the house. I sat and tried to ignore the screaming. I'd given up worrying about what the neighbors thought.

I tried to figure out what to do with myself. Although I was anxious to finish my book, I knew reading would be out of the question. I grabbed my phone and a pair of headphones and tried listening to soothing music. It helped a little, but I made a mental note to ask for noise-canceling headphones for Christmas.

He isn't even trying to pretend he likes me today. But that's OK because right now I don't really like him either.

Immediately, I felt guilty.

It was the first time I allowed myself to be that honest. Anytime the negative emotions rose up, I pushed them down. After all, good moms liked their kids all the time, and I wanted so badly to be a good mom.

The guilt made me mad. The expectation to love him unconditionally felt unfair.

Who would WANT to be treated this way? Who would enjoy being around someone who was this mean to them? If he were an adult, people would think I was crazy for putting up with this. If he were an adult, I'd tell him to get the hell off my property or I'll call the cops, so why do I have to put up with this just because he's a kid?

I had always connected love with warm, fuzzy feelings. For two years, I was the mom who was always hugging my kids. I heard that you don't hug wounded kids because they're huggable; you hug them to help them become huggable. Lately, I had to force myself to even hug them goodnight.

Does that mean I don't love them?

I thought back to what the kids' therapist had told me. She said when families stopped feeling guilty for disliking their challenging child, she could finally make progress with them. She told me multiple times I had to let go of the guilt and understand that I *did* love my children. I was attempting to do what was best for them, regardless of the personal sacrifice.

At some point, she even asked me, "Have you killed any of them?"

I laughed. "Of course not."

"Have you left any alongside the road?" She winked at me.

"No."

"Well, you're doing pretty well, I'd say." She leaned back in her seat and chuckled.

I thought back to that conversation and continued to reason, *I don't **feel** like I love him, but if I didn't love this kid, he wouldn't be in my home for sure. He'd have been kicked out a long time ago. For that matter, all three would have been gone.*

Parker finally stopped banging on the door and sat on the stoop until it was time for him to leave for his behavioral class.

Dreams of Parenting

A few weeks later, I spent an evening hanging out at my friend Kara's house while Lynn was at home with the kids. As we chatted, Kara's six-year-old daughter ran over and leapt into her arms.

"I love you, Mommy!"

"I love you, too!" Kara gave her daughter a big kiss on the cheek.

As I watched this girl jump into her mama's arms with such love and abandon, it was too much for my soul to bear. Shortly after, I excused myself and left for home, weeping the entire time. I arrived home, thankful our kids were already in bed, and cried as I told Lynn about it.

"I know this may sound selfish, but tonight I found myself wishing and longing, for just a little bit, to have a 'normal' child — a child who would love me back, who doesn't hate my guts, and who isn't constantly manipulating me. It makes me sad to think I may never have the kind of relationship that I want to have with the kids."

"I'm so sorry, Jennie. I know this is tough."

From the time I was young, I had dreams about what parenting would be like. I always imagined chubby little toddlers running up to me, leaping into my arms, happy to see me when I picked them up from Grandma's.

As they grew older, I pictured pushing them on the swings in the park as they squealed with glee. I could almost hear the joyful noises in my head as they ran through the sprinkler on a hot, summer day or came inside to find I'd made their favorite treat.

I knew things wouldn't be easy, but I still had dreams about having a great relationship with my kids. I looked forward to fun girl times with my daughter, connecting in meaningful ways while we shopped or painted our nails. I imagined watching my son play baseball, cheering his team on to victory with great talks afterwards over McDonald's french fries. I longed for a time when we would all sit around the table, having fun and laughing, playing games like Life or Trouble, or going on fun family vacations.

Reality seemed more like a nightmare than a dream, as I dealt with the gut-wrenching possibility that I might go through all this torment and heartache only to have my children completely reject me and make choices that would destroy their lives.

The loss of that dream relationship was more than I could bear. I found myself grieving what could have been, though at the time I didn't know I was grieving. Sometimes I felt extremely sad or irritable without understanding why.

I started to recognize my need to grieve when I found myself feeling jealous of parents who were raising more typical children. I would sit at the park and watch moms hug smiling kids, and my heart ached. I felt the same sting of pain when I watched other families sit in a restaurant laughing and having fun as I dealt with an angry child who was acting out.

I also felt jealous of others who seemed to have easier, more comfortable lives. When jealousy began to creep in, I recognized it as a sign that there was something I needed to grieve.

Getting Help

Ever since his school routine had changed, Parker was getting so out of control at home that the kids and I couldn't do many of the fun after-school activities we had previously enjoyed. He created so much chaos that the other two, who had been settling down, amped up their behaviors when he was home.

Going to the gym most days was out of the question. It was nice outside, but a simple walk resulted in Parker trying to trip one of us or throw rocks at Bri or Stephen. Unable to engage in normal activities, I felt like a prisoner.

I usually bought groceries or ran errands while the kids were at school, but now I barely had time to run to the grocery store before it was time for Parker to come home. Sometimes he could barely handle being in the living room. I was stuck.

There were days when it was so hard to get to the bathroom that I had to wait until Lynn got home to go. On Parker's better days, I would send the kids to their rooms and go to the bathroom.

Taking advantage of those breaks, I savored moments of peace and quiet, taking in a few deep breaths. It amazed me what five minutes of resting and breathing could do for me, even in the middle of the chaos.

We had only been on the new schedule two weeks, but the entire family was exhausted. Since the other kids were settling down while Parker was still out of control, we decided to send Parker to respite. I felt bad sending him away, but I knew his behaviors and needs were too much for any of us to deal with all the time.

Megan, our social worker, found Ann and Trent to do respite for us. Because they were farmers, they agreed to watch the kids during seasons that didn't interfere with harvest. They watched the kids once a month, October through December, and a few other times. For the first couple of visits they took all three kids, which was heavenly.

We found it hard to find people who could handle our kids' behaviors. Some offered to help, but they had young children, and we didn't want to run the risk of the younger kids getting hurt by our three. When we met Ann and Trent, they didn't have any children of their own, although they later had three.

This strong couple did well with our kids. We found we could sit back and relax for a few days without having to deal with any crisis or put out any fires. Ann and Trent put our kids to work alongside them.

Rather than the "party" many other respite providers gave the kids, this couple provided exactly what they needed: to have less fun away from us than they had with us. Otherwise, they came back to us with such huge behavioral challenges it didn't feel like we got a break.

After the second time watching the kids, Ann told us, "I think we can only handle two kids at a time."

It was hard to find two separate places to send the kids when we needed a break from all three. For a while we worked to find a third person so the kids could all go to respite, but we eventually sent Parker by himself because having him out of the house for a weekend was such a huge reprieve.

As I dropped Parker off and drove away, I felt myself relax. Sadly, despite not having Parker there, we had a terrible time. Everyone was on edge. We were all decompressing from having to deal with his increasingly challenging behaviors over the past few months.

CHAPTER 12

Working Toward Forgiveness

That Sunday as we walked into church, I thought about how difficult everything had been and about the doctor's advice to reduce my stress level.

I tried to smile back at the friendly faces that greeted me, but that required too much energy. I tried to avoid talking to anyone, but a friend caught me in the foyer.

"How are the kids doing?"

Although I appreciated her concern for the kids, I was struggling so much that I needed someone to ask me how *I* was doing. Even though I couldn't quite articulate how I was doing, and I probably wouldn't have been fully honest, it would have been nice to be asked.

As we walked into the sanctuary, I looked at the stage with curiosity. Normally well-lit, the stage had been transformed, with stage lights darkened and garbage strewn about.

As soon as worship started, my eyes welled with tears, and I had to stop singing several times. I was able to pull myself together until they sang "This is Amazing Grace."

Who brings our chaos back into order?

Who makes an orphan a son and daughter?

The King of Glory, the King of Glory!

That song got me every time.

Despite my own struggles with our adopted kids, the idea of adoption still tugged at my heart. I knew it was dear to God's heart, and it was still dear to mine.

After worship, Jeff, the youth pastor, talked about how we gradually allow garbage into our lives and find ourselves in darkness. As he spoke, God spoke to me.

God showed me the garbage in my life, the things that were weighing me down and keeping me in a dark, painful place — bitterness, hurt, unforgiveness, and self-pity.

I had allowed the hurt to remain in my heart as a sick, twisted badge of honor.

God once again made it clear to me: my kids weren't going to change. They were stuck in their own issues. I loved my husband dearly, but there were times he couldn't understand what I was going through with the kids when he wasn't with us. And that wasn't going to change.

The whole time I was whining at God to change my circumstances, He had been pointing me to the truth that the only person I could change was me.

Later that week, I was reading *Living Successfully with Screwed Up People* and came across these words, "Failure to forgive locks you into a self-focus that pleads for restitution and revenge... True forgiveness stores indiscretions and wrongs in the file under the heading 'No Longer Relevant Except for Lessons'... Forgiveness allows us to grow as a result of lessons learned and prevents hardening of the heart from bitterness."

I had just heard about it Sunday in church, and now it called to me in black and white.

"All right, all right, God. I get the message."

As I realized how much I needed to forgive, it dawned on me that I needed to forgive God. He hadn't done anything wrong, but I was holding on to resentment toward Him. I felt that God had asked me to do an extremely challenging task and then abandoned me. I felt betrayed, and I struggled to trust Him. If He put me into this situation, how could I trust Him not to do something like that again?

I thought back to the day I told Him I didn't want to talk to Him anymore because He had asked us to adopt Parker. I had pushed Him out of my life, but now I realized I couldn't get through this without His help.

One of the things that made forgiving my children difficult was that I felt like a monster for harboring ill feelings toward them. It was a struggle to admit how much they had hurt me, and although I logically knew they were behaving out of self-protection, I still resented their behavior and needed to practice forgiveness.

In my mind, forgiving them would undo the seriousness of all they had done to me. If I forgave, it meant they hadn't done anything wrong. If I forgave, all my battle scars were for nothing. They would get off Scot-free, and I would be stuck dealing with the results.

I held on to resentment because I felt it justified keeping my kids at an emotional distance. I didn't have to continue getting hurt by them; I could keep them at bay and avoid having my heart repeatedly torn into pieces.

In the end, I learned it was quite the opposite. When I held on to even a little bit of bitterness, that was when I became stuck, like a fly wrapped in a spider's web. Satan had me right where he wanted me. He could use the kids' past offenses to continue to wound me.

> *Forgiveness is about the victim not being victimized two times: first by the wrong, then by a misguided requirement to hang on to the wrong. Forgiveness is about freedom to live above the hurt and to go on with joy in your heart, in spite of the injustices. . . Forgiveness is a determination to be free! I won't let what someone else does destroy me, regardless of how I am affected. Whether you forgive or not has nothing to do with the seriousness of the abuse or wrong; it has everything to do with whether you want to be free or prefer to carry the burden.*
> —Elizabeth Brown
> *Living Successfully with Screwed Up People*

The next day as I read those words, I knew God was trying to drive home the message of forgiveness. I wanted the freedom I had experienced in the past, yet I struggled to maintain this mindset.

Putting the Fun Back in Dysfunctional

When I went to pick Parker up from respite, Ann and I stood in the kitchen while he collected his things. "You wouldn't believe what Parker did while he was here . . ."

I held my hand up. "I'm going to stop you right there." I knew she wouldn't be offended. "Is this something I need to know because I need to do something about it, or is it something you dealt with here and I don't have to know? I'm not at a place where I can hear about anything he did that I don't absolutely need to know. I'm barely making it as it is."

Ann laughed. "I understand. It's not something you need to know. But I do have to tell you something else, because you'll get a kick out of it. Trent and I love how creative you are with discipline, so we've been using a lot of what you do with your kids with our little guy, even though he's only two. We even came up with a saying we ask each other before we decide what to do."

"Oh yeah, what's that?"

"WWJD. Most people think it stands for 'what would Jesus do,' but in *our* house it stands for 'what would *Jennie* do.'"

I laughed. "That's a scary amount of pressure, but THAT is hysterically funny."

The next weekend, Lynn took the kids to Seattle to give me a break and picked up a good friend of mine on the way back.

I met Angie years earlier when I lived in Wisconsin. I was thankful she decided to spend a week with me. Angie was a dear friend whose zest for life was as contagious as her beautiful laugh. Having her in my home was wonderful, and it felt good to laugh with her and share my life.

Angie sat next to me on the couch. "You should write a book."

"You think so?"

"Oh, my goodness, Jennie. Already your kids have come so far. You've gone through so much with them! At the very least you should write down things as they happen, so you can look back and remember how it was."

When I was a small child, I told my mom I was going to write children's books, and my brother, who was artistic and loved to draw, would illustrate them. I had even written to the author of *Uncle Arthur's Bedtime Stories* to tell him I planned to write children's books just like him.

While I wasn't sure I would write a book, I started journaling and writing down more of the situations I experienced with the kids, just in case I ever decided to.

Angie saw a few of Parker's meltdowns, and it felt good to have one more person understand what my life was like. Brianna and Stephen acted like perfect angels that week, so she didn't see as much of their normal behavior.

Angie's visit went way too fast. Brianna went with me to take Angie back to Seattle, and before Angie's departure, we took her to the Space Needle and other attractions. We took pictures of the three of us doing crazy things like pretending to be spies as we snuck through parking garages. I hadn't been that silly in years, so it felt good to be my old self again.

More Laughter

After Angie left, I thought about the difference having a little fun had made. I walked away from my time with her feeling recharged, ready to face the week.

I need to infuse more laughter into my life.

I thought back to the first time I understood the power of fun and laughter. A couple of months after Brianna and Stephen moved in, Lynn's mom offered to watch the kids. Lynn and I jumped at the chance to have a little time to ourselves. The kids were typically better behaved for other people, so we knew she would have no problems.

We found what looked like the funniest movie at the time and bought tickets. We were the loudest people in the theater, practically rolling on the floor, laughing hysterically as if each humorous line was the funniest thing we'd ever heard. I noticed people looking at us, but it felt so good to laugh I didn't care.

The movie we saw, *Wild Hogs*, starring Tim Allen, John Travolta, Martin Lawrence, and William Macy, might have been as funny as we thought, but we were so over-stressed and tense that we would have laughed at anything. In any case, I came back from the evening of intense laughter feeling refreshed, ready to go back to helping my kids heal.

I wish we'd kept doing fun things. I realized I felt bad for having fun, especially when the kids seemed so mad and sad all the time. Plus, any time I allowed myself to enjoy something, the kids would freak out and try to bring my attention back to them. At some point, I had decided it wasn't worth the hassle to keep trying.

After Angie left, I came across a quote that challenged me in *Living Successfully with Screwed Up People*: "Each of us is about as happy as we decide to be."

It reminded me of something I read by Victor Frankl: "The last of the human freedoms is to choose one's attitude in any given set of circumstances."

He wrote this from a Nazi concentration camp.

A short time later, I scrolled through Facebook and stopped at a picture of someone holding out their arms in the middle of a rain storm. The quote made me stop and think.

> *"Life is not about waiting for the storm to pass. It's about learning to dance in the rain."*
>
> — Vivian Greene

I wasn't dancing in the rain. I was pouting in the middle of a mud puddle.

I spent a lot of time planning for how I would enjoy life "when..."

"When the wailing fits stop, I will be able to enjoy life."

"When Brianna stops trying to triangulate, I will have a good relationship with my husband."

"When other people understand me, I will be happy."

"When the kids move out, I can relax and enjoy life."

That one made me the saddest. I didn't want to wait that long to enjoy life.

Then it hit me. I was allowing my children's issues to set the course for my life, allowing them to dictate who I was going to be.

I'd seen it happen in so many families. Fun seems to be the first thing to go when a family is parenting a severely wounded child. I had watched fellow parents become so engrossed with their child's pathology that they ceased living life in a healthy manner.

I realized I was doing the same thing.

Before kids, I was a happy person. I enjoyed belly laughs with friends, and people were always commenting on my "contagious smile."

Part of my struggle was thinking that if I allowed myself to be happy, it was like admitting the situation wasn't going to change. If I stayed miserable long enough, I could somehow force my situation to change. I had also begun to believe this sad, lonely, tired version of myself was the true me.

My kids were looking for guidance. I couldn't let their anger, fear, and sadness dictate the atmosphere at home. I needed to learn to dance in the rain, even if it felt more like a monsoon than a gentle drizzle. Otherwise, we weren't going to make it.

CHAPTER 13

Puppy Love

My desire for a small dog came as a surprise to me. I had always been a large dog kind of girl. I hated yippy little dogs because they annoyed me with their constant high-pitched barking.

After all the post-move craziness, I desperately felt the need to have someone return my love. Lynn didn't always understand my anger and frustration with the kids, and I frequently felt utterly alone. I craved the unconditional love of a dog. We already had Captain, who would have been a lap dog if he could, but it's hard to snuggle a 150-pound dog. I couldn't stop thinking about getting a real lap dog.

After simple kindness from a gas station clerk caused me to cry uncontrollably in my car for more than fifteen minutes, I gingerly brought up the idea of getting a small dog, hoping Lynn would agree. At that time, he wasn't interested in having another mouth to feed, and I didn't have the energy to push it. While I understood his point, I couldn't shake the desire to have a dog in my lap, snuggling with me or licking my face while we watched TV.

My parents visited us that April, when we'd been on Parker's new schedule for about three weeks. As soon as I saw them coming through the airport, I felt a load lift off my shoulders.

Three days after my parents arrived, Mom and I went to Walmart to grab a few things for dinner. When we finished shopping, we noticed a litter of adorable little pups in the grass at the end of the parking lot. As we admired the puppies, I wanted one so badly but resisted the urge to bring one home. As much as I wanted one, I didn't know how Lynn would feel about me buying a puppy after we'd already talked about it.

When we got home, I told Lynn about the pups.

"Jennie, we already talked about this. We don't need another dog in the house. One big dog is enough!"

I dropped the subject, and Mom and I put groceries away and planned dinner. Soon after, Lynn left to grab something from Home Depot.

After an hour I looked at my mom. "What is taking him so long?"

"I don't know. You'd think he'd be back by now."

I later found out he had heard God telling him, "You know she hardly ever asks for anything. Go get her one of those puppies."

After taking off, supposedly to Home Depot, Lynn proceeded to purchase one of the pups and everything I would need for him. As he walked into the door, carrying both dog and accessories, I was ecstatic. As excited as I was, neither of us had a clue how much I would need that dog over the next few years.

I named the pup Sport, and he soon became a source of normalcy for me. When he saw me coming, he wagged his tail in pure joy. As I petted his tummy, he licked my hand in thanks. I had become used to being punished for loving, but this little dog reminded me what it was like to have love returned. Even little things, like a wag of the tail or sitting by my feet to snuggle, began to restore my broken heart.

The only challenge that came with the dog was the kids' jealousy. They still struggled if I gave attention to anyone or anything besides them, whether it was a niece or nephew or an animal. They freaked out much more than I anticipated. Both boys separately told me they were mad enough to kill the dog, and they made comments anytime I played with Sport.

"You love the dog more than us!" they'd exclaim.

Eventually, I got tired of hearing it and responded sarcastically with, "At least the dog is nice to me."

Kill You with a Fork

I could tell Bri was angry. Grandma and Grandpa were gone, and it was back to just me and the kids after school. I pulled her onto my lap as the boys played where I could see them.

"I hate you, and I want to kill you."

"Why do you want to kill me?"

"Because Dad got YOU a puppy and not me."

I looked over at Sport, my little sanity-saver, who spent time in his kennel while I worked with the kids on their homework or any other time I couldn't supervise their every move with him. I looked back into my daughter's big, blue eyes. I noticed the black of her pupils had almost overtaken the blue, which was usually an indication of distress in her.

"I'm sure that was tough for you."

"Yeah." She looked down. Despite the rest of her answers being short, I was proud of her. Usually it was hard to get even one word of real emotion out of her.

After talking through her feelings for a while, I asked Brianna, mostly out of curiosity, "So, how are you going to kill me?"

"With a fork!"

Knowing she wasn't serious about killing me, I laughed.

"Sweetheart, if you're going to kill someone, you may want to use something a little more effective, like a knife or a gun," I jokingly advised.

"I could do a lot of damage with a fork!" Brianna gave a sheepish grin.

"Well, I know you're having a tough time, so here's a kiss with my love in it." I playfully kissed her on her cheek.

"Nuh-uh." She moved her sleeve across her cheek. "I wiped it off."

"My love is strong. You can't wipe it off. You just spread it, and now you have my love on your arm, too!"

With a look of disgust, Brianna wiped her hand on her pant leg.

"Now you have it all over your legs!"

"No! I wiped it off!"

"Not my kisses. The love from my kisses is strong, and it sticks to you. You can't do anything to get it off."

Watch Someone Die

Brianna wasn't the only one talking about death. One afternoon as Parker was in his behavioral class, his morning tutor called me.

"Jennie? I don't know how to tell you this, but I'm concerned about Parker."
I noted the shaking in her voice. She was obviously distressed.

Oh boy, what did he do now?

"Parker and I were discussing WWI in our history lesson." She hesitated.

"OK...?"

"Well he turned to me and told me, very coolly, 'I think it would be really cool to watch someone die.'" Her voice was so shaky by now I could hardly understand what she'd just said.

"He said he thought it would be cool to watch someone *die*?"

"Yes."

"Oh, OK." Part of me wasn't surprised at all. But another part of me was shocked.

"I thought you'd want to know about it." Her voice was almost a whisper. "It was more the *way* he said it that freaked me out."

My heart sank.

I knew what she meant. A couple of weeks earlier, he had talked about wanting to be the Joker in Batman, ". . . because he looks like he's having fun all the time."

Something in the way he had said it made my stomach churn, similar to how I felt about the kids' obsession with roadkill.

While his behaviors made it incredibly challenging to even want to work with him, the fear that he might one day hurt somebody motivated me to keep trying to help him heal. I mostly feared that the person he eventually would hurt would be me.

It was hard for me to even look at him that afternoon. I was already frustrated because of what he'd done the previous week.

Just the week before, Parker had gone even slower than his normal speed-of-an-iceberg, walking with baby steps to the van as he watched the family members who were waiting not-so-patiently for him. Lynn needed to get to work, and Brianna and Stephen were already late for school. To speed Parker's steps, Lynn spun the wheels of our minivan, hoping to light a fire under Parker's feet and let him know he was about to leave if he didn't move faster. He finally slumped into the van.

Later, when I picked Parker up from his tutoring session at the library, he limped along, dragging one leg behind him in a way that made Igor look like an Olympic athlete. I took a look at his pathetic hobble and said, "Knock it off and walk normally."

I'm sure the angels rejoiced as his leg miraculously healed and he immediately walked without a trace of the former limp.

I found out later he'd spent the entire day telling everyone his dad had "run him over with the van." Luckily, the school professionals knew us, and knew Parker's tendency to lie. He almost convinced a bus driver to call CPS. Then the driver spoke with Parker's teacher and learned that false accusations were a common occurrence for him.

I found myself thankful for the lessons I'd been learning about forgiving and letting go.

Stephen's Favorite Teacher

I sat across the table from Lisa, Stephen's teacher, as we sipped our coffee.

"He's started acting really mean towards me," she said.

Lisa had quickly become Stephen's favorite teacher, and with good reason. Lisa had invested a lot of time into helping him do well that year. A kindred spirit, she and I had become good friends and occasionally met for coffee to discuss ways to help Stephen, as well as life in general.

"I'm so sorry to hear that. It's because he likes you and he can see the end of the school year approaching. He's pretty good at using passive-aggressive ways to let people know he's struggling."

She laughed and nodded. "Oh yeah, he has been refusing to do what I ask him or pretending he doesn't hear me when I talk to him."

"That's a fun one, isn't it? It drives me nuts. And when I confront him, he denies he's doing anything on purpose."

"I figured it was because of the end of the year, but isn't he starting pretty early?"

"He really likes you. Basically, it's his way of saying goodbye. Aren't you glad he loves you so much?"

She smiled. "How can I help him?"

"Start telling him you're going to miss him, too. I'll work with him at home to look for a healthier way to say goodbye. Maybe I'll have him make you cards."

"I'd appreciate that. It's getting tough to work with him because his behavior is getting louder and louder."

"That's exactly what he does. My husband thinks I'm crazy for confronting him on the tiny, passive-aggressive things, but if I don't catch it when he's acting out in small ways, he gets louder and louder until I address what's going on underneath. I have to do a little 'therapy session' with him or have him write in his feelings journal so he can express his feelings. It's hard for him."

"I'll try explaining to him that I know why he's misbehaving and see how that works."

We sat quietly for a moment, and I changed the subject. I needed to talk about something other than the kids for a while.

CHAPTER 14

Mommy Shopping

Sally and Gabe, a couple in our small group, invited us over for a cookout with a bunch of their other friends. As we walked in, I could feel exhaustion weighing on me.

I watched Bri scope out the place and zone in on the sweetest-looking lady in the crowd. Within minutes, she was cuddled next to her on the couch, sucking up like a Hoover vacuum.

Even after two years, her mommy shopping hadn't slowed much.

Many of my fellow adoptive moms also lamented about their children wanting anyone besides them. A friend of mine shared that one day, as she was looking through Facebook, her daughter sat looking over her shoulder. When she saw one of her mom's friends, she said, "I want HER to be my mommy."

As Lynn and I spoke with Sally and Gabe, I watched out of the corner of my eye as Brianna took snacks over to the lady and went back to snuggling into her side.

A friend of Sally's walked into the kitchen where we stood, and Sally introduced us. "Jennie and Lynn, this is my friend, Jana. Jana, these are our friends, Lynn and Jennie. They've adopted three foster children."

"Oh, that's so cool. Do you have any real children?"

While I understood what she was asking, the way people worded those types of questions made me feel like a second-class mom. Of course I had "real" children. Two were playing in the room beside us where I could see them. One was snuggling on the couch with a complete stranger. My sense of humor rose up. Did she want to pinch my kids to see if they were "real"? I held my tongue.

"We don't have any *biological* children." I was hoping she'd pick up on the nuance of my answer.

We continued talking, but about thirty minutes into the party, I noticed the dear, sweet woman Brianna was sitting next to had started shooting me hateful darts with her eyes.

Oh, boy. Who knew what Brianna had been telling her. Like Parker, Brianna had a history of making false accusations.

As I pondered the various options of what this poor lady might have heard, the intensity of her glare made me think that perhaps Brianna had stepped up her game. Brianna must have either convinced her I was the Wicked Witch of the West – or worse – the Devil incarnate. Either way, I was convinced it included me eating little children for lunch and picking my teeth with their shoes.

The sad thing is, under different circumstances, I bet this woman and I could have become good friends. She had kind eyes and a laugh that made me think I'd have enjoyed getting to know her.

I heaved a huge sigh, excused myself from the conversation, and went into the living room.

"OK, Brianna, you need to come and stay by me," I told her, ignoring the dirty looks from the woman beside her. Brianna would need to spend the rest of the party stuck by my side.

Back in the kitchen, as Bri melted into my shoulder, Jana commented, "I can tell your family is close."

I smiled. If only she knew.

He's Not Ready for Middle School

As the end of the school year approached, we needed to make a decision on Parker's next grade level. Mrs. Pratt was making huge strides with him, but it was obvious that he wasn't ready for middle school.

We sat in a year-end IEP (Individualized Education Program) meeting, trying to figure out what to do. Representatives from Southgate, the school he had attended since arriving, Cascade, where his new behavioral class was located, and Park Middle School, which he was slated to attend the following year, sat around the table.

"We need to figure out how to best help Parker," said Loraine, the special ed representative from Park Middle.

"In order to do that, we have to keep in mind he's smarter than all of us combined," said Mrs. Pratt. Everyone laughed and gave knowing nods.

"The problem is, we don't have a program for kids with this many behavioral issues," said Loraine. "He will have to attend a day program in the Psych unit at Lourdes Hospital next year."

"What is the program at Lourdes?" I asked.

"It's a half-day program that focuses on behavioral issues."

"A half-day! What will happen with his education?" I didn't even want to talk about him being home even longer each day than he had the past few months. I was hanging onto my sanity by a thread!

"Well, it's not ideal but that's the best we have."

I looked around the room, infuriated.

"Does anyone feel like he is ready for middle school?" Karen, the school's psychologist, asked.

Everyone shifted in their chairs and mumbled, "No."

I took her comment and ran with it. "Then why are we pushing him through to the next grade? This is ridiculous!"

"Well," the principal of Southgate said, "we don't practice holding children back."

"*What?* What if they need to be held back?" Lynn grabbed my hand under the table, signaling I had gone too far.

"It's just not something we do," she said, matter-of-factly.

"Isn't there anything else available?" Lynn quickly said, as if he felt the need to speak up so I wouldn't.

I took a deep breath and spoke before anyone else had a chance to, "Look, it's obvious he isn't ready to move forward. Mrs. Pratt is doing such a good job with him. He has a situation that's good for him, where he can heal. Why push him on just because it's not policy to hold a child back?"

"Well..." the Southgate principal began.

"We'd be willing to hold him back." The principal of Cascade stood up as he joined the conversation. Everyone looked at him.

He continued, "When you moved, you moved into Cascade's territory anyway, so we would be willing to transfer him over to Cascade and hold him back another year. We can move him back to a half-day in Katie's classroom and a half-day in the fifth grade general education classroom."

I sat back in my seat and let out a sigh of relief. I looked over at Southgate's principal and saw her sigh, too. I wasn't sure he was ready to go back into the general ed classroom, but I said nothing, afraid that if I did, it would all go away and we'd be back to the nightmare of having him home for a half-day.

"I'd love to work with him again," said Mrs. Pratt. "Parker has a lot of potential."

"Thank you," Lynn said, finally letting out a sigh of relief himself. "We appreciate the hard work all of you have put into helping Parker, and we are so thankful for your help."

"Yes, THANK you," I said, tearing up as I looked over at Cascade's principal. "Thank you so much!"

"It's my pleasure."

Keeping Busy

On the days Parker could handle it, I took the kids to every fun event I could find that summer. It was becoming more difficult to find activities for older children. There were already activities Brianna couldn't do because she would be starting middle school soon.

They tended to be the oldest kids at most events. I could tell some made them feel uncomfortable at first, but the kids warmed up quickly since the events fit their emotional age.

We went to the splash park. We attended a Kid's Workshop at Home Depot, where they got to make a wooden tool carrier. We saw Valentine's Performing Pigs at the library. Their 17-year-old pig, Nellie, had performed on *Animal Planet*, *David Letterman*, and other TV shows. We watched the pigs jump through hoops, dance, and push a play lawnmower.

We also went to free movies at the theater. They were among the few times that I could relax while with the kids, because they were mesmerized by the big screen for an hour and a half. Even then I couldn't let my guard down completely. Extreme supervision was still necessary.

Even after two and a half years, the start of every trip began with an intense and panicked, "Where are we going?" from each of the kids. I knew it was normal for children who'd been through trauma, but it caused me to feel constantly on edge.

When we stayed home, the kids still needed structure, so I began posting the day's schedule. They moved from art projects to games, quiet reading times, Lego time, or perhaps Brain Gyms and chores. I hoped they could follow it without much guidance, but that was rarely the case.

Since Parker had been home so much during the spring, it wasn't far into summer that I felt myself wearying. My patience was running thin. Money was tight. We couldn't afford to send the kids to day camp like we had before. I sent them to the Boys and Girls Club twice a week when I could.

With so few breaks, I began to slip back into old patterns of not taking care of myself, and it showed in the way I treated my family.

Despite my growing impatience, I worked hard to provide a lot of positive reinforcement and pizazz for good behavior. I made such a big deal about any good choice that I inadvertently taught the boys to open doors for me as we walked into buildings.

"What a gentleman you are!" I said with enthusiasm when one of the boys imitated Lynn by opening a door for me.

From that time on, the boys would practically kill each other in a bloody battle trying to be the "gentleman" who opened the door.

My Own Private Horror Film

"I don't know what's wrong with you," Lynn said one evening on the way home from a date night, "but the kids are fine."

I looked outside the van window into the twilight, feeling like I'd been stabbed. I often felt more harshly judged by Lynn than by any outsider.

I shifted my weight in the passenger seat, unsure of what to say. The fire of anger rose in me, but fatigue pushed it back down. Despite the lack of energy, I forced words out.

"Was I like this before the kids came to live with us?" I glanced over at his silhouette.

"No!"

"Well, do you think they might have something to do with it?"

Lynn said nothing.

It didn't feel fair. We were in this together, but it hardly felt like it. The kids treated us differently. Lynn could leave his things around the house, and they'd rarely be touched. If I did the same, my things were stolen or broken. Lynn could leave for a couple of days, and no one acted up when he returned. At most they acted out their frustrations toward him on me. If I went away for a couple of hours, I returned to weeks of payback behaviors.

It felt like I was in the middle of a dark, sinister horror film, where the main character knows what's going on but can't seem to convince anyone there's danger.

In some ways, I understood why he thought I was the problem. Although the kids had always treated him differently, this pattern intensified after Parker was kicked out of the regular classroom.

I'd been trying to take better care of myself since my trip to the doctor, but having Parker home more and experiencing increasingly mean behavior from all three made it impossible to maintain a positive attitude toward them.

Earlier that day, Lynn left for work with a chorus of, "Bye, Daddy," ringing in his ears, complete with Parker batting his eyelashes. The moment the door closed, Parker turned around, the look on his face making *Poltergeist* look like an animated children's movie. "Now you're in for it," his face said.

Like every other day, I dealt with outrageous, crazy-making behaviors from all three until Lynn returned. Then they made a 180-degree turnaround.

"Oh, Daddy, you're home!" Parker would say, his voice dripping with sugary sweetness. The others would join in, as if angels in a choir. Their over-the-top sweetness made me want to punch someone.

Lynn would come back to the kitchen, where I was fixing dinner while practically twitching, growling, and foaming at the mouth. Frustrated at the change in behavior, I'd bite his head off.

What he saw was that the kids were sweet to him; I was the one acting out my anger toward him, snapping and blaming his laid-back approach to parenting for causing conflicts for me. I'm sure it didn't make sense that three innocent children could push a grown woman so close to a nervous breakdown.

The only reason my husband knew I'd had a hellish day were comments from me – usually some sarcastic form of, "Oh, Daddy, we were *angels* all day!"

The kids pitting us against each other was excruciatingly painful. Lynn had been my rock. Now he felt like my enemy, or at least someone who was siding with my enemies. I'm sure he wondered if a crazy person had inhabited the body of his once-loving wife.

I didn't even know how to get him to see the bizarre dance the kids were doing. I tried to explain what was going on, but it barely made sense even to me. Sometimes I felt like I *was* losing my mind. I'm sure it looked from the outside like I was. I was barely surviving, but it didn't look as if our marriage was going to.

There were times I felt jealous of Lynn. He could do no wrong in the kids' eyes, while I could do nothing right. It was difficult for them to differentiate between me and anyone who had let them down in the past.

For them, it was safer to take that anger out on me while treating Lynn as if he'd hung the moon. It was easier for him to have fun with the kids, because he wasn't dealing with their constant barrage of negative emotions.

It never felt fair. I couldn't catch a break. I found myself resenting Lynn.

Once Lynn asked the kids why they treated me so terribly compared to how they treated him. They talked about being afraid of him. He was a man and much bigger than they were. They feared he would hurt them if they mistreated him.

They also said they felt safer with me and talked about how I was the primary person helping them heal, and how that process was scary to them. One admitted that it scared him how good I was at figuring him out and picking up on his games.

"You're Mean!"

It had been a rough day. I'd been trying to practice self-care, but by the middle of July, my head was barely above water. I was back to just trying to survive.

As usual, the kids demanded non-stop attention. They constantly asked questions they knew the answer to and struggled to do anything on their own. Stephen had been particularly challenging and passive-aggressive, pretending he didn't hear me when I talked to him. Finally, I'd had enough.

"GO TO YOUR ROOM! I'm SO DAMNED TIRED of this!"

"You're *MEAN!*" Stephen yelled. I stopped in my tracks and turned around.

"I'M mean? *I'M* mean? Am *I* as mean to you as *YOU* are to ME?"

"No," he said, matter-of-factly.

"OK. When I'M as mean to YOU as YOU are to ME, then you can complain!" I walked away.

I hated that I had I lost my temper, but I was tired of the kids' "I can treat you like poop, but you'd better be nice to me" double standard.

The next day was Saturday, and the entire family went to our niece's birthday party. I kept a close eye on Parker, making sure he wasn't hurting the younger kids, as I chatted with an acquaintance.

"How are things going?" she asked.

"I'm exhausted. Parker couldn't handle being at school for a full day, so he was home a lot. He's having hour-long wailing fits on a regular basis. Sometimes he's so out of control we can't even go for a walk without him trying to trip or throw rocks at us."

"Well, just remember God won't give you more than you can handle."

Stifling the urge to smack her, I smiled and nodded. I knew she was trying to make me feel better, but I was tired of people making unhelpful, patronizing comments. As soon as I could, I found a reason to slip away and walked over to grab a drink.

I thought about what she'd said and wondered why it bothered me so much. Though I'd heard that platitude most of my life, it didn't seem to ring true. I felt like I was about to break, and I knew God had put me in this situation.

In the beginning, when someone said that to me all I could think was, *I wish He didn't think I was so strong.* The more I thought about it, I began to believe that sometimes God allows us to be in challenging situations to show us how much we need Him and to remind us that He has our back.

At least, I hoped so.

CHAPTER 15

Broken Things

"OK, boys, you need to stop messing around and get up from that chair. It's really important to me because my grandparents refinished it, and they aren't alive anymore."

As soon as the words "it's important to me" escaped my mouth, I wished I could catch them and stuff them back down my throat before they hit the boys' ears. I knew how this would end.

After a brief pause to look at me, Parker thrust his legs back and the chair crashed backwards, breaking and twisting its fragile legs. Time seemed to speed up around me. All I could do was watch it crash to the ground as I responded in slow-motion.

I thought back to the first time I made the mistake of telling the kids something was important to me. A few months after Brianna and Stephen's arrival, they sprayed their hair blue and gold for spirit week.

"Hey, Mom! Can we borrow a mirror so we can see the back of our heads?" Brianna asked.

The only hand-held mirror I owned wasn't much to look at, just a black, plastic mirror with a circle of white, fake gems on the outside corner. Many spots sat empty where gems should have been. Had the mirror not held sentimental value, I'd have tossed it out already.

Naively, I handed them my treasure. "This is very important to me, so be careful with it."

Moments later, they returned the mirror to me in several large, broken pieces. I felt sick to my stomach, knowing they'd broken it on purpose. I sent them to their rooms and called my mom, becoming a blubbering mess as I recounted the story.

My mom gently chided, "It's only a mirror, Jennie."

"I know, Mom, but I loved that mirror. When I was a little girl I would sit and watch you use it. I remember thinking how pretty you looked and how I couldn't wait to use the mirror while I put on makeup, just like you did."

"But it's only a mirror. People are more important." Everything about my mom touted that philosophy.

"But they did it on purpose. That's what makes me so mad!"

"Jennie, it's only a mirror."

Now, seeing the chair I loved in pieces, I wanted so badly to call my mom and cry to her, but with a two-hour time difference, I knew she and Dad would already be in bed.

Instead, I wrote in my journal:

"Anything I love gets destroyed. Anyone I love besides them gets hated, so I feel like I can't love anything."

I called my mom the next morning and told her the story.

"Parker was sitting on Grandma's old... um... her old... wait a minute. What do you call that thing you sit on?"

"That thing you sit on?" Mom started, puzzled, "Ummmm... do you mean a 'chair'?"

"Yes! That's it."

Mom chuckled.

"I don't know what's wrong with me lately, Mom. I can't seem to think of simple words. It's like my brain isn't working properly. I can't remember appointments. In May, I missed a meeting at school because I forgot. It's getting frustrating."

"I wish I knew what to tell you."

I sobbed.

"Mom, I can't do this. I don't think I can make it one more day. Can you please come here and help me? I really need you right now."

In all honesty, I'd needed her for a long time, but I'd been trying to be strong.

"I'll be there as soon as I can."

It was a month before she got there, but having that to look forward to was enough to get me through in the meantime. I needed my Mommy.

After I got off the phone, I thought more about the issue of forgetting things. *My memory is terrible. I don't think this is normal.*

I decided to go back to the doctor. In some ways, I'd started to feel better from taking the vitamins, but there was much more happening. I had been feeling depressed, to the point of not wanting to get out of bed. The kids' therapist had suggested I go on an antidepressant, and I resisted. I visited an M.D. the week before, but even though she'd prescribed an antidepressant, I hadn't taken it. She had spent two minutes with me, thrown me a prescription for an antidepressant, and left.

I wanted a second opinion.

My insurance had changed and no longer covered the naturopathic doctor I'd seen back in February.

Maybe I should look for a naturopathic doctor my insurance covers. As I looked at the list, I saw two. One was a guy. I wasn't comfortable seeing a male doctor. I decided to make an appointment with the other, a Dr. Judith Caporiccio.

"Get This Child the Hell..."

"Get this child the hell out of my house!" I barked into the phone.

That swear word was mild compared to the other words going through my head at the time.

"I've been thinking about what happened this morning. It wasn't an accident that

Parker kicked the dog into the wall. I can't live with a child who does that. I just can't."

I had been telling Lynn for a while that I worried about Parker being around Sport, but he'd dismissed it as paranoia. That morning, Lynn promised he would watch the dog while I took a shower. I was getting dressed when I heard a loud yelp from the living room. Lynn was with the other kids in the family room, when Parker did something to the dog. Lynn ran into the living room and found a whimpering little dog that could barely walk and a boy who said, "Oh, it was an accident."

Later, Parker admitted to Lynn that he was trying to get Sport into the other room to kill him. When the dog ran, he panicked and kicked him into the living room wall.

Lynn, now on the other end of the line, replied, "Now, Jennie, let's talk about this."

He stopped himself and, pausing, added, "What do you need from me right now?"

"I need you to get over here and deal with this child. I can't today. What he did went way over the line of what I will handle. Plus, Sport has been acting funny ever since it happened. I need to take him to the vet."

In many ways this dog had become my saving grace, helping me recover some shred of sanity. At times Sport was the only family member besides Captain who seemed to be happy to see me. His unconditional love had allowed me to get through mounds of smeared boogers, urine-saturated carpets, broken treasures, and bad attitudes. Someone hurting him on purpose threw me into despair.

Lynn was silent for a moment. "I'll be right there."

For my husband to take time off work was a big deal, especially with the Boys and Girls Club's summer programs in full swing. He knew I was done.

I sat there, after having already sent the kids to their rooms before making the call, and contemplated my options. I couldn't send Parker back and, deep down, I knew that's not what I wanted. He was already adopted. I knew he was meant to be a part of our family. I made the commitment to be his mom. The thought of getting rid of Sport for his own safety caused me to weep bitterly.

When Lynn arrived, I bolted out, carrying my precious cargo and anxious to hear what the vet had to say. My deepest fear was I would have to put the dog to sleep. Straining to see the road through my tears, I drove to the vet's office.

I'm sure I looked a mess when I walked in, fearing the worst, but I was relieved when they told me that Sport was OK and kennel rest was all they recommended.

I wrestled with whether to re-home my beloved pup. After all, it wasn't fair to him.

"Seriously, God. How can you ask me to do this?" I cried the entire way back home, then pushed the idea out of my mind. I couldn't stand the thought of getting rid of my little ray of sunshine.

My Pit of Despair

I begged God to get me out of this situation. I loved my husband, but this was not what I had signed up for.

I longed for heaven. I was tired of living in a world where little kids got hurt and acted out that hurt on the people trying to help them. For the most part, I wasn't suicidal, although one night after Lynn and I got into a fight, I briefly considered driving the van into the river.

I wanted the pain to go away. The world felt less and less safe to me every day.

I thought about Jesus' words before He was crucified: "My Father! If it is possible, let this cup of suffering be taken away from me. Yet I want your will to be done, not mine." Matthew 26:39, NLT

I wasn't quite able to say, "Your will be done."

There were times when I begged God for another way out of my predicament. I figured if He wasn't going to take *me*, He could take the kids. Sometimes when Lynn and the kids were out, I prayed God would cause a car accident and only take the kids.

Other times, when Lynn and I weren't getting along, I half-jokingly told God He could throw Lynn into the mix, as well. I looked at the pain and hurt we had all endured and begged Jesus to come back and take us all to heaven.

Daily life carried on. Lynn and I went on a date the next week. We ate at

Applebee's, then headed for the new Transformers movie, laughing as we strolled into the theater holding hands. Afterward, we walked through Walmart, grabbing a few items we needed before heading home.

"I liked this movie better than the first one. They had amazing graphics," I said.

"I agree. They do a good job with special effects."

I looked over at Lynn and realized how much fun I had with him. Briefly, life felt normal – a stark contrast to the battleground in which I lived. I pictured us running off to Bermuda, lying on a secluded beach, or living on a sailboat. My feet developed a mind of their own and stopped on the pavement, as if stuck in wet cement.

Please don't make me go back, I repeated over and over in my head.

Lynn, unaware of this battle going on behind him, got in the car. After what seemed like minutes but was probably only seconds, I forced myself to get in the car. I silently repeated the phrase but dared not say it out loud. It sounded terrible, even in my head.

Later that night, Lynn came back to our bedroom to find me packing, tears streaming down my face.

"What's going on?" His voice was full of surprise.

"I'm out of here. I can't do this anymore."

"Whoa! We just had an amazing date. Why would you suddenly decide to leave?"

"That's the problem. I had fun. And with what I'm dealing with day after day, the thought of going back into this is unthinkable. All I wanted to do tonight was scream, 'Please don't make me go back!'"

"There's got to be something we can do."

"If I stay, something has to change. I can't do this anymore."

That night I had a conversation with God:

"Lord, you know I have always wanted to follow you, no matter where you led me, right? I need you to know I'm tempted to even walk away from you to make this pain go away. I'm not quite there yet, but the temptation is real."

While I know Lynn was struggling during this time as well, I was hurting too much to even be aware of it. All I knew was I was a wreck. I wanted to take the next train out of town and run away from it all.

Over the next few days, Lynn and I brainstormed what we could change. We decided Lynn would stay with the kids more on weekends so I could have a break. I would have preferred to leave the house with Lynn instead of by myself, but there was no other choice. We also decided to take a break together so we could strengthen our relationship.

Chapter 16

The Slap

A few days later, already on the edge, I was trying to get ready for the support group meeting that night. In the middle of the bustle, Stephen, who had a terrible attitude the whole day, mouthed off to me.

As if I was having an out-of-body experience, my arm flew out, and the palm of my hand contacted the side of his face. Horrified that I had just slapped my son, I sent him to his room so that I could cool down.

I didn't hit him hard, but I felt terrible.

I had never slapped or even physically punished a child before. I prided myself on being in control, patient, and loving. I had no idea I could lose it like that. I felt like a failure as a parent. I knew I had to let go of it and forgive myself, and I needed to ask Stephen to forgive me.

When Lynn got home, we all went to the support group meeting.

After we returned home, one of the other moms called me.

"I thought I'd let you know what Bri told all the kids tonight at support group."

"OK..." I said, hesitantly. There was no telling what she had said.

"She told everyone you slap her whenever she disagrees with you."

"You've got to be kidding me," I said with deep sigh. "I'm sure it had to do with me slapping Stephen earlier today, but that's the first time I've ever touched one of the kids."

"I'm sure it does. As soon as my daughter told me I thought of what you shared tonight. I'm so sorry!"

"It's so frustrating."

"Well, I explained it to my daughter, but I thought you might want to know what Bri is saying."

When I got off the phone, I told Lynn what my friend had said.

"I'll deal with it," he said, then called out, "Brianna, I need you to come here for a second."

When she came into the kitchen, he said with a sly smile, "I understand that mom slaps you whenever you disagree with her. I'm concerned for your safety; after all, your evil, out-of-control mother might fly off the handle and slap you again. I'm going to protect you by having you stay in your room. I love you too much to risk your safety."

Bri eventually told him she made up the story in retaliation because I'd gone out with a friend earlier that week.

Brianna's lies irritated me, but slapping Stephen gave me a wake-up call that even the trip to the doctor hadn't. Seeing that my lack of self-care was affecting my parenting made me realize I needed more help.

The kids' therapist had become an important support for me, providing me with empathy and understanding, and letting me know my emotions were normal, but it wasn't enough.

Whenever we got home after therapy, I struggled to function well. After finding out what my kids had gone through, I felt ill-equipped to deal with my own wave of emotions. I didn't know then that hearing about another person's trauma could create something called secondary, or vicarious, trauma.

I scheduled an appointment with a counselor, hoping she would understand, even though she didn't work with wounded kids.

Date Week

Toward the end of July, Lynn and I arranged for the kids to attend camp so we could get away together. The boys would go to Royal Family Kids Camp, a Christian camp specifically geared toward children involved in foster care. Our time away would be longer than their time at camp, so they would stay with their Aunt Debbie until camp started, then with Ann and Trent after camp ended until we returned.

Bri, now too old to attend the same camp, would go to a week-long horse camp.

Lynn and I wrestled with the decision to send Brianna to a "normal" camp.

"I don't know, Lynn. She's more likely to get away with unhealthy stuff at this camp. They're not trained to deal with her behaviors, and she'll be really sneaky."

"I know, Jennie, but what else can we do?"

Finally, Lynn decided. "There is no perfect solution, Jennie. I know she may do things that aren't healthy for her, but we NEED the break!"

I thought about what the kids' therapist often told me: "Jennie, you can't fully protect them from the world, and you can't fully protect the world from them."

What she was saying was true, but I still tried to shield the kids from making poor choices. I knew Lynn was right; our sanity was more important than keeping Brianna sheltered.

After getting Brianna settled at camp, Lynn and I headed out for our vacation. Our first stop — and the most relaxing of the three — was Lake Quinault Lodge, a charming hotel built in the 1920s that seemed to have been frozen in time. As I looked into the mirror above the pedestal sink, I imagined women in chiffon dresses and cloche hats standing where I stood.

Neither of us wanted to leave, but we were scheduled for our next destination the following night. The cabins at Kalaloch Lodge sat along the ocean. We walked along the beach, looking at starfish and the piles of beautiful driftwood.

We only had one night scheduled in the cabins and had an extra night before the next stop, so we brought a tent and slept in a small campsite on the beach. We hiked into the woods and looked at old, hollowed-out trees with holes large enough to walk in.

The last resort we'd pre-booked, Sol Duc Springs, was more like a trailer park than a vacation destination. The small, unimpressive cabins were surrounded by natural springs that fed into pools that were overcrowded and noisy. After an hour at the pool, Lynn and I, tired of being splashed by loud children, spent the rest of our time in the little cabin.

In the past, I'd have given anything to hear the sounds of children happily playing. Now, even joyful noises irritated me and made me sad that we had waited so long to get this break.

After our night at Sol Duc Springs, we still had a couple of days before picking up Brianna at camp. Lynn and I decided to continue up the coast and explore a bit more.

As we drove into Port Townsend, I fell in love with the sailboats in the marina and the quaint downtown. We booked a hotel room and walked around town. The various shops and fliers for cultural events made it obvious that many artists lived there.

As I sat on the porch of our hotel overlooking the marina that night, I found it difficult to relax. Everything in me wanted to drink in the beauty and enjoy the time with my husband, yet I felt restless.

The next day we sat on the pier, enjoying a treat from Elevated Ice Cream and Candy Shop. They had many unusual flavors, but I landed on lavender mint. Lynn, as usual, chose the ice cream with the most chocolate. He has always said that anything that isn't chocolate isn't worth the calories.

As we looked out over the water, I fought the temptation to think about challenges and pushed down the dread I felt about going home. I forced myself to listen to the rhythmical waves crashing onto the rocks below and the seagulls shouting out their hellos. I took in the smell of the ocean, fully feeling the weight of a cool breeze pressing against my face.

Back in our hotel room, I wrote down a quote I'd once heard. I would post it at home so I wouldn't forget.

> *"Only in quiet waters things mirror themselves undistorted.*
> *Only in a quiet mind is adequate perception of the world."*
>
> — Hans Margolius

Why Is She Being So Weak?

Lynn's schedule changed in August when he became the Children's Pastor at our church. He began to attend the kids' therapy sessions with me. One of the first times he came, he asked the therapist, in reference to me, "Why is she being so weak?"

His question devastated me. With everything I was going through and the way the kids played him against me, most people would have already been in divorce court. I felt betrayed, hurt, and misunderstood.

It was an honest question. His word choice wasn't the best, but he was trying to communicate his confusion over his normally strong wife now seeming to be a puddle on the floor. He was asking, "Where did my wife go? She's usually able to handle a lot."

Her face showed a mix of irritation and confusion. "If your wife wasn't as strong as she is, you guys would be divorced, and Parker would be back in foster care. Lynn, just so you know, almost every spouse that comes into my office says the same thing. Usually it's something to the effect of, 'Gosh, we raised four beautiful children, and my wife was fine. Now we have adopted Princess here. Princess is doing fine, but my wife has gone crazy.'"

Lynn still didn't get it. "But sometimes they are nice to her, so I don't get it."

"You're right. Sometimes they are nice. But it's not often enough to outweigh all the mean things they are doing. When you're at work, do you ever get kudos for doing your job well?"

"Yes."

"When your wife does a good job, most of the time she gets the opposite response. The kids may give back from time to time, but for the most part all your wife gets back from them is negativity. That's hard to deal with day in and day out and still feel positive."

As I listened to her, more of my experiences made sense.

New Ways of Healing

I dropped the kids off at the Boys and Girls Club and headed for the first appointment with my own therapist.

"What do you do for fun?" the therapist asked.

I'm sure my blank stare was a dead giveaway that I had honestly forgotten how to have fun in the middle of all the chaos. The kids' needs so overshadowed my own that I hadn't even thought about doing anything for my own enjoyment in a long time.

Aside from occasional dates with Lynn, there was the visit from Angie and a trip to Portland with my sisters-in-law, but on a daily basis, fun wasn't even on my radar.

What did I do for fun?

She continued, "I'd like you to come up with fifteen to twenty smiles, meaning things that bring a smile to your face. It can be as simple as taking a walk or a bubble bath, but it needs to be something you enjoy."

The task seemed insurmountable, but as I worked on my list I felt a little more like myself again. It was good to remember what I loved to do.

"OK, now that you have your list, I'd like you to *do* one or two of the items EVERY day," she said at our next appointment.

"It was hard enough to come up with the list. You have no idea what my life is like. I don't have *time* to do anything for *me*."

"I know it feels impossible, but I'd like you to try. It doesn't have to be elaborate, but I want you to do one thing for yourself every day."

Doubtful, I took my list back home. One of the items on my list was "play guitar," something I hadn't done for a long time. I pulled out my guitar and started playing.

Sure enough, as soon as I was doing something that didn't involve the kids, they acted out for attention. I'd end up only playing one song before I had to quit, but I couldn't believe how good it felt to do something – anything – for myself.

I didn't know at the time, but choosing to do something enjoyable every day would be a key move toward my emotional health. It reminded me who I was, without my children's pain and anger distorting my view like a circus mirror. It allowed me to take challenges in stride, without my feelings getting hurt or my spirit being sunk.

THIS is My Doctor?

Dr. Caporiccio entered the room. I noted her neat appearance, which contrasted so drastically with the first naturopathic doctor I'd seen. A short woman in her late fifties, she wore a long-sleeved dress made of sturdy, gray fabric, with a flap around her neck. Her graying hair stood in a bun, covered by a stiff, translucent white bonnet.

Her friendly face quickly put me at ease. Her exam was thorough, and her gentle eyes, full of concern, seemed to bore through me.

"How are you sleeping?" she asked.

"I'm sleeping better than I was before, but I'm still not sleeping through the night."

In between answering questions, I sat there, trying to figure out her background. She entered my answers into a computer, so I didn't think she was Amish. Later, I'd discover she had become a German Baptist in her 40's.

"How are you doing emotionally?"

"I'm definitely dealing with depression."

"Have you been put on any medications for it?"

"Well... I was given a prescription for an antidepressant by a medical doctor, but I wanted to try a more natural route, so I've been taking St. John's Wort."

"I want to find out if there are underlying medical reasons for your depression, but it's pretty clear you need to start taking something." Her gaze made me wonder if my emotional struggles were written so obviously across my face.

There was something about her manner that made me trust her. She talked about getting tests done, and I liked her research-based approach. If she thought I should be on an antidepressant, I needed to try.

Besides, the kids' therapist had begun begging me to get on one.

I had always viewed taking medication as something people did when they couldn't handle life and needed a crutch, but that was changing.

Dr. Caporiccio told me that while my depression didn't begin as an organic issue, it had become one through the trauma I had experienced with the kids. Pathways in my brain had been altered, and they wouldn't be changed back without help. Exercise and other tools could be useful, but I was too depressed to even think about exercising.

"I'd like to do a basic blood work panel. I'll have them include your vitamin D levels, because vitamin D deficiencies can be an underlying cause of depression." She looked over to make sure I wasn't getting overwhelmed before continuing.

"I'd also like to test your cortisol levels to make sure you should be taking Seriphos and, if so, determine the correct dose. You have a lot more going on, but we won't worry about that now." She handed me the cortisol kit and gave me instructions.

I did feel overwhelmed, so I appreciated her taking it slow.

"I would like you to make sure you're on a good fish oil and a whole-food multivitamin right away."

I made a mental note to stop at the supplement store on the way home and felt relieved to see her writing her recommendations down for me.

"Along with the antidepressant, I want you to take a natural sleep aid and another that will require a prescription."

As the appointment neared an hour, I found myself wondering if we were keeping another patient waiting. I liked that she was so thorough and looked for underlying causes for the symptoms I was experiencing. I found out later that she practices Functional Medicine, which looks at the whole person instead of isolated symptoms.

In years to come, "Dr. C" would become more like a friend than a doctor. Little did I know, this kind, spunky lady across from me would help me climb out of the pit where it felt like I was living.

CHAPTER 17

Best Birthday Ever

Because of how terrible Parker's birthday had been the year before, Lynn and I decided to try something new. It fell on a Saturday that year, so we wouldn't have to worry as much about his behavior in school.

In the weeks leading up to his birthday, we said little about it. When the day arrived, we pared down the celebration to bare bones. We decorated with one small banner rather than the normal streamers, balloons, and other decorations. We didn't get fancy birthday plates and barely even said "happy birthday" to him.

We ate dinner with just the five of us, gave him a few presents, and had a simply-decorated cake, without the usual ice cream and other snacks.

I felt bad giving him such a lame birthday. Even though we based our decision on what we felt was best for him, I wished we could have done more.

That Monday afternoon, I got a call from Parker's teacher.

"Parker was so excited about his birthday," Mrs. Pratt said. "He raved about it all day."

"Really? I was feeling guilty we'd given him such a terrible birthday party!"

"No, he told me, 'That was the best birthday ever!'"

I got off the phone, shocked. I was learning that for him, less was often more. At the time, I didn't understand over-stimulation and sensory overload, which are common in both children with autism and those who have experienced trauma.

Quieter and simpler often works best for them.

As I practiced simplicity throughout the school year, I found he responded well to it.

I also took the "less is more" approach to physical affection with him. Despite my fatigue, I had tried to give him lots of hugs to help him bond.

"Stop hugging Parker," the therapist finally said.

"But aren't I supposed to be trying to bond with him?"

"Some kids can't handle getting close. I think he may be one of them."

"How am I going to help him bond, though?"

"You'll have to give him short, quick displays of physical affection, like high-fives or touching his shoulder."

I learned that he did better with these "drive-by" displays of affection. They didn't overwhelm him, and his behavior quieted. His anxiety lessened, and the house became more peaceful.

No One is Doing Anything Wrong

That fall, Lynn started going to therapy sessions with me so we could work through our marital struggles. The therapist told us, "No one is doing anything wrong; it's just that what you're doing isn't working."

Her advice helped us look for solutions rather than blame. It was no one's fault there were hurts in the marriage. We were in a tough situation. We could allow the situation to tear us apart, or we could use it to build a stronger marriage. We chose the latter.

While Lynn said he understood what I was going through, I believed he either didn't understand or didn't care that I was hurting. I finally had to accept that he really couldn't know all that was happening.

Lynn was responding to how I turned into Mr. Hyde when I struggled. I inadvertently communicated bitterness and hatred, but the underlying issue was extreme exhaustion and a lack of needed support. From his point of view, I was the one being mean to him, not the kids. Understandably, that left him hurt and confused.

What I didn't realize at the time was that I rarely shared raw emotions with him. When I became more transparent and shared my inner struggles, he began to understand.

Lynn and I also learned that to help the kids heal, we had to work as a team. From early on, I was more the disciplinarian, while Lynn was more the "fun guy." I wanted him to be stricter. He wanted me to lighten up. Neither of us was doing it wrong – we just weren't on the same page. I needed to let go of some of the rules. He needed to step up more.

We decided that we would always support each other in front of the kids, even if we disagreed with a decision the other had made. We would talk about issues away from the kids but present a united front. We tried to follow through on consequences the other parent had given, though we didn't always remember or agree.

We also tried to work together to determine what we would and would not allow the kids to do, and we talked through discipline options together. If one of us felt more strongly about a rule than the other, we worked toward a compromise.

To make things easier, we developed a system to prevent the kids from triangulating between us, and to prevent either of us from getting tired of making decisions.

When we were both home, we divided the decision making. Lynn answered questions related to technology and screen time, while I answered questions related to food, such as if they could have a snack or dessert. On questions about special events, like going over to someone's house, we decided together.

I also learned that when I got tired, I needed to depend more on Lynn to help me figure out how to discipline a child. Since he wasn't in the middle of it and hadn't had to give out twenty consequences already that day, he had more clarity and objectivity than I did at that moment, so I began calling him to get his input.

Our working as a team gave the kids more consistency. It discouraged them from triangulating. When we didn't work well together, it showed in the atmosphere

---

around the house. The more we worked together, the better it was for all of us.

Lynn and I also tried to prioritize a weekly date night. During our date, we were not allowed to talk about kids. Although at times we broke that rule to talk through important issues, we felt much closer when we focused our energy on each other.

At times we had to get creative for our date nights. When we couldn't find child care, we improvised. Sometimes we put each child in their own room with dinner and some sort of electronic device – something they rarely used and weren't normally allowed. We would spend the evening in the living room and enjoy a candlelight dinner, complete with dessert and a movie.

When we spent time with each other on a regular basis, it kept misunderstandings from festering.

CHAPTER 18

Sure, Push My Buttons

I read a striking sentence from *Living Successfully with Screwed Up People*: "Buttons are the danger signals that warn us of unresolved problems."

I became obsessed with figuring out how not to let the kids' behaviors affect me. That meant more research. I turned to John Townsend's book, *Who's Pushing Your Buttons*.

In his book, Townsend says:

> *A difficult person can exhaust the good feelings and attitudes we need to have toward her. Years and years and many negative experiences often drain the love you once felt for the person. The resultant thoughts are something like, 'I am broken inside about her. Let someone else handle her; I can't generate positive feelings for her anymore.' This is understandable, and it is good to recognize this. You aren't a bad person when you can no longer feel the outflow of love you once had. It is more a state of emptiness than a mean or selfish state.*

I was discovering that love was doing what's best for another person regardless of how we feel. Feelings of love may come later, but ultimately love is how we treat the other person.

While I sometimes felt bad about my love coming from a decision of the will instead of a feeling, I realized it was OK. It was unrealistic to expect feelings of affection. Since I was dealing with such challenging behaviors all day with few of the typical joys or rewards of parenting, warm feelings would have been unusual.

Especially in difficult relationships, true love comes down to decisions over feelings.

Marriages that last rarely do so because both people feel fireworks going off at every moment. More often it's because they choose to stick it out, despite occasional urges to abandon the relationship. My grandparents were married for sixty-five years. They used to joke, "We never thought about divorce. Murder, yes, but not divorce."

Being released from the requirement to constantly enjoy my children or to feel loving toward them in order to believe I was a loving parent took the pressure off of me. I also realized that if I didn't care about my little "button-pushers," they couldn't get to me like they did. I could spiral myself into some major guilt trip, but my love for my children was great, even if it didn't look like that of other moms on Facebook.

I had given my life for these children, choosing for years to treat them well, regardless of how I was being treated. Did I make mistakes? Certainly. There were times I didn't behave with love, but I chose to stay, to push on and commit my life to their wellbeing. THAT was love, no matter how it felt.

Supernatural Help

I desperately needed God in order to love my kids well. My own, human love was long exhausted.

I worked through Daniel Siegel's book, *Parenting from the Inside Out*. He said that parents must resolve their own past trauma to do the therapeutic parenting needed to help a child heal.

His words motivated me to keep track of what triggered me the most and process the *why* behind my triggers. What emotions did they bring up? What message was I getting from them, and what past trauma did they bring to the surface?

When my kids acted out their rage, it triggered my intense fear of other people's anger. Dealing with an angry person made me feel like a kid, trying to figure out what I did wrong. Even hearing someone yell at another person made me incredibly uncomfortable. I grew up assuming that if someone was angry with me, I was automatically responsible.

Parenting children with high levels of rage and anger forced me to look at this fear. It taught me that I couldn't fix someone else's anger, nor was it my job to do so. I learned to ask myself, "Is this my problem or theirs?"

Occasionally, I had let them down and apologized for doing so. However, most of the time their anger was obviously misplaced. That made it easier for me to learn the difference. Even though it was directed at me, it usually had everything to do with what happened to them in the past.

While mentally I knew this, it became clear that I could deal with their big feelings without taking on responsibility for those feelings. Gradually, I got better at it.

The Gift of Pain

It is natural to focus on the apparent cause of our distress. But this is a distraction. Our real focus should be on ourselves. We need to look at our own feelings and our own responses to difficult people's behaviors. We need to ask ourselves why we are reacting so strongly... I find it useful to think of the difficult people in my life as being like skilled tennis opponents or tough professors. I don't like what they do, I don't like how I feel, but I recognize that they provide me with an unmatched opportunity to improve myself, one that is available nowhere else.

— Mark Rosen, *Thank You for Being Such a Pain*

My children's issues gave me an incredibly beautiful gift. They helped me recognize areas in my own life that needed to be healed. My children's pain highlighted my own pain in a way nothing else could have done. They became a mirror by which I was able to see cuts, bruises, and smudges I'd wanted to ignore.

It was a challenge to find time and space to deal with these issues, but doing so helped me tremendously. As I was able to deal with my own issues, I was better able to help my children.

My children's efforts to control their surroundings forced me to face my own lingering control issues.

I had struggled with knowing what to do when people tried to control me. For the first twenty years of my life, I handled it by letting others decide things for me. In high school and through the first few years of college, if a friend asked where I wanted to eat, I said, "Wherever you want to go." In my early twenties, I realized this wasn't healthy and started to change.

I had come a long way, but in many ways I still let other people determine what I should or shouldn't be doing. I worked hard not to let them control the environment, but too quickly gave the kids control over my emotions.

As painful as it was, in dealing with my own issues I took some of that control back. After all, wounded children can't push buttons that aren't there.

I did not find it easy, but I discovered that if I looked at the children's bothersome behaviors as an opportunity for extreme growth on my part, I could handle situations much better.

> Remember that the biggest issue is not solving your crazy-making connection; it is your life and growth. Never lose sight of that. Your button-pusher may have been the trigger, or catalyst, that got you in touch with your need, hunger and brokenness, as is often the case. On the other end of things, your growth and health will flow into new ways of being and relating that can greatly help matters.
>
> —John Townsend, *Who's Pushing Your Buttons?*

Angels Arrive

As I frequently did, I took the kids to the park after school to give them a chance to run off steam. Tonya, our new care provider – the answer to my mom's prayers – joined us.

The kids still spent more time trying to demand my attention than playing, but it was exciting to have Tonya's help in pushing them on the swings and redirecting them when they made poor choices. I could tell she was going to be a huge ally in helping with the kids after school.

A local agency had approved our application and given each of the kids 32 hours per month for care providers. We went through a couple of others before finding Tonya and Jackie, the gal who helped in the mornings. They quickly became angels to me.

After some playtime, I gathered up the kids and said goodbye to Tonya. As I drove along the narrow road away from the park, a little gray and white pup sat in the middle of the road, scratching her ear, unfazed when I blasted the horn.

"This dog is NOT moving. It's going to be run over if someone doesn't grab it," I said.

"I'll get it!" Bri exclaimed. In her world, you could never have enough shoes, soft blankets, stuffed animals, and – especially – dogs.

I didn't have a chance to think about it before Brianna jumped out of the van and snatched the puppy. She was back in the van before it even dawned on me that this might not be safe.

The puppy was young, maybe four or five months old, and was just skin and bones. When we got her home, she barked nonstop at the other dogs. If you raised your hand or moved your foot around her, she would yelp and jump away, obviously afraid of being hurt.

I remembered something I had felt God telling me a week earlier. "You're going to get another dog."

"Yeah... right. We already have two. We DON'T need another one," I replied, and forgot all about it.

I didn't know how wrong I was.

Since the puppy wore a blue collar, we searched for an owner. After a week with no response, Lynn posted pictures on *Craigslist*, hoping to get rid of the dog. But this endearing little pup had wormed her way into the rest of the family's hearts.

"There's a family coming to look at the puppy in about thirty minutes," Lynn said to me.

I didn't have the energy to fight to keep her. He had already compromised by getting Sport.

I sat in the living room petting this sweet dog, trying to spend as much time as I had left with her, as tears streamed down my face. Brianna overheard him and ran to the bathroom, loudly crying.

Ten minutes later, I heard him on the phone.

"I can't do this. My family is too attached. I'm so sorry, but we are going to keep her."

The new pup and Sport became inseparable. Captain was getting older, and his energy levels didn't match theirs. Before this new puppy came along, Sport would jump around Captain, who played for a short while then held Sport down with his front paw to let him know he was done.

Emma — this gray and white, skin-and-bones, little Jesus-with-fur, loving dog— soon became a comfort to me. Her eyes melted places in my heart that were cold. Her gratitude made up for the entitled attitude I faced with my children. As you petted her, she looked up with chocolate brown eyes full of love and gratitude. You could almost imagine her saying, "Thank you for saving me." After a short time, she would grab your hand with her paws and pull it to her mouth, so she could thank you with a lick or two.

I wondered if this precious dog was an angel in disguise, because her love was like water to my parched soul. It was as if God placed her in the middle of the road and told her, "Don't move," knowing I wouldn't have picked her up unless it was a matter of life or death.

Everyone loved Emma. Even my dad, who isn't much of a dog person, was tempted to sneak her off to Wisconsin after visiting us. This sweet, timid, easily-frightened dog healed my heart with every lick of her tongue and loving gaze of her eyes, even as we helped to heal hers.

Too Much Helping

Toward the end of September, Lynn and I brought our kids and recruited half a dozen other Forever Homes support group members to help one of our families with their large yard.

This family was in the middle of the licensing process to become foster parents. Lynn and I could tell the process was wearing them out, so we decided to support them by helping with yard work.

After raking some leaves, I leaned on the rake and looked around the yard. As I stood there, watching the others work, I became acutely aware of my exhaustion, and all I could think of was our own yard, which sat in complete disarray.

Why haven't you slowed down? I chided myself. You're tired and here you are, helping someone else do yard work. Don't you remember what the doctor told you?

As I forced my hands to move the rake, I decided that I had to stop helping everyone who asked. I wanted to be there for the other moms in the trenches, but I simply couldn't. Moms would call to meet with me, and as they shared their difficult stories, I found myself struggling to listen without feeling overwhelmed. That didn't help my attitude toward my own children.

My raking slowed as the realization sank in. *I can't keep this up. If my body shuts down, I won't be any good to anyone, including my own children.*

Later that night, I talked to Lynn about my revelation, and he finally agreed that I should stop meeting with moms. I breathed a sigh of relief that he finally seemed to understand how much I dealt with each day with the kids.

"You'll still work on the benefit concert, though, right?"

"Of course. I'm going to see it through."

Lynn and I put on the benefit concert in November, and it was a wonderful success. We'd also been asked to speak at Heart for the Fatherless, an adoption conference, the next day. I had hoped to take Brianna to a conference for teenage girls called the Revolve Tour, in Portland, but it was the same weekend. I knew it would be good for her, so I decided to take her to the one in Sacramento the next weekend.

Sacramento with Brianna

As we pulled out of the driveway, I was aware of my bad attitude.

I'd given and given to Brianna, and the only thing she gave back was sass. I gave up hope that she would ever come around. She had broken my heart way too many times. It felt like the blood, sweat, and tears I had poured into her the past couple of years were all for nothing.

Her choices broke my heart, becoming so high-risk that, as I thought about her potential future, I felt only dread and sadness.

I had pushed myself too hard before the adoption conference and concert, so I was sick again. The doctor had determined my cough came from a viral infection, not pneumonia, so I decided to go.

After we'd driven awhile, I grabbed the sandwich Brianna had made for me that morning, amazingly without any eye rolling, huffing, or complaining. Not only did she have a great attitude while making the sandwiches, she took a Sharpie to my sandwich's bag and drew a heart on it. It was the first obvious display of love I'd noticed from her.

When we arrived at the hotel, we had a little bit of free time before the event started.

"What sort of interesting things are there to do here?" I asked the desk clerk.

"Honestly, there's not a lot to do. The only thing I can think of is shopping at the mall."

I looked over at Bri and saw a huge smile spread across her face. Shopping was her favorite thing in the world, as well as her biggest trigger. I braced myself but decided to take her.

As we hung out at the mall, I noted how far she'd come.

She no longer tried to run ahead or fall behind as we walked through the mall. It was a little easier to get her to talk and interact. Some of her edge had tapered off, and it was the first shopping trip where she hadn't hinted for anything.

At the conference, Bri was mesmerized by the lights and music. I even detected a slight smile, which was something that didn't happen very often.

I sat there exhausted but enjoyed the music. Group One Crew finished, and Hawk Nelson took the stage, playing worship songs.

As I looked at the crowd, I sharply felt my own emotional distance from God. Everyone around me seemed to enjoy the worship, except me and of course Brianna, who at that point didn't seem to want anything to do with God. Despite my pain, I lifted my hands and began to sing, finally letting myself worship.

Almost immediately, I heard God speak to my heart.

"You've given up on her. But I haven't."

I teared up. It was true.

God's words convinced me to look beyond the present circumstance, which gave me hope to believe that despite how things felt at the time, He was at work behind the scenes. His words gave me the strength to keep going.

Bri laughed as the speaker talked about relationships. I sat there, hoping his words would sink in and affect the way she interacted with boys.

Later that night, when we returned to the hotel, Bri looked at me and said, "This was the BEST day of my life!"

I smiled. That moment of unprecedented gratitude made the weekend worth it. It seemed God was saying, "Look – all your hard work is paying off."

The next day we enjoyed more music, speakers, and skits. I saw Bri smile more than she had in a long time. I enjoyed being with her so much that I decided to extend the trip and take her to San Francisco on the way home.

In the morning, we drove across the Golden Gate Bridge on our way to Fisherman's Wharf. Bri especially loved the street performers on Pier 39.

We grabbed huge chocolate sundaes from Ghirardelli Ice Cream and Chocolate Shop and rode the trolley to the main shopping area. Brianna loved the trolleys where she could sit on the outside and hang on to the poles. She was behaving responsibly, so I let her have more freedom. We walked around, looking at the high-end shops. Everything was way too expensive, but we had fun window shopping and exploring, then headed home late in the afternoon.

After this trip, I noticed Brianna softening, though the changes were subtle. Criticisms she once would have stated loudly for others to hear became quieter and kinder.

"You have something in your teeth," she'd whisper to me, not wanting to embarrass me. Jabs came less frequently, and she started to leave sweet little "I love you" notes for me and Lynn.

Much of what seemed like baby steps for my children were really huge leaps. In tiny increments that I often overlooked at the time, my children were healing.

I Like to Move It, Move It

The next Saturday, the kids and I spent some time over at my friend Jill's house. She was part of our Forever Homes support group.

She and I were trying to talk. The other kids were playing where we could see and hear them. Andrew, her adorable, curly-haired two-year-old foster son, played with the other kids, while Travis, his five-year-old brother, performed the only part of a song he knew for his audience.

"I like to move it, move it. I like to move it, move it. I like to move it, move it. I like to move it, move it."

Like many of my own children's performances, something about it seemed off. It didn't have the ring of a child singing for enjoyment or to have fun. It felt forced and manipulative.

Back in the car after our visit, I sighed in relief, glad to be away from the impromptu concert. I no more than turned the key when all three of my kids started singing, "I like to have attention, I like to have attention."

The kids called out what seemed to be Travis' underlying motivation. I saw it as progress that they could see it so clearly in others, but I chuckled under my breath over how often they failed to see their own behaviors as attention-seeking.

As my kids continued to heal, not only did they become much better at recognizing their own emotions and reactions, they also became experts in picking up on those emotions and issues in others. They would come home and say, "Suzie could use a good mom like you. She has anger issues," or, "That kid needs to see our therapist, Mom."

I joked with Lynn that we were training three little counselors.

CHAPTER 19

Extreme Self Care

Browsing through its pages, I knew I needed to purchase *The Art of Extreme Self-Care* by Cheryl Richardson. I wasn't sure about buying it, because I had been taught that love meant putting others before myself.

During my own childhood, I learned that my needs were not as important as everyone else's. Messages sent in sermons seemed to reinforce that idea. I interpreted this to also mean that I should only meet my own needs after I met everyone else's.

But by now, I knew better. I had to stop living on emotional fumes and fast food.

As I read Cheryl's book, I became very aware that my level of self-care didn't match my extremely stressful situation. I was getting better at taking care of myself, but self-care was usually the first thing cut when stresses increased.

I'm not taking care of myself like an Olympian.

I resonated with her about the importance of having a place of beauty. I dreamed about creating such a space.

I knew beauty could be incredibly healing, and I needed a sanctuary, since my home had become a battlefield. Our bedroom was small, and we couldn't do much to redecorate it. I wondered what could be done with the large room off our family room.

"What if we painted this old 70's style paneling?" I asked Lynn one night. "It would still be wood paneling underneath, but maybe it would look nice with a coat of paint."

"Don't you think it would be a waste of time? Eventually we will tear the paneling down and put in regular walls. Shouldn't we wait?"

"Who knows how long it will be before we have the energy or the money to do that? We don't even use that room because it's so ugly."

Lynn finally agreed, and I set out to choose a color. Parker had thoughtfully chosen a beautiful, decorative box for my last birthday, and I wanted to use it as the centerpiece of the room. I took it in and matched the paint as closely as I could to the seafoam green on the box.

I took a lot of breaks while painting the room, but as the seafoam-colored paint slowly covered the old paneling, a complete transformation took place, and we decided to repurpose the room from an office into my art studio.

After I finished painting, I carefully chose aqua-colored accent decorations and soon, thanks to Craigslist, we had a small sitting area where I could play guitar and read.

"This room is huge. It needs something else," I told Lynn.

"What about a craft table in the other corner where you can do art?"

"Yes! That's it!"

As the studio continued to take shape, it became a cherished space. I loved the way light radiated through the large, open windows. There was a cozy chair, and an inviting Takamine guitar I'd purchased from my brother years before sat in the corner, waiting for me to dust it off and play a few tunes.

Brianna gave me the softest blanket known to man that Christmas, and it made its home on the country-blue couch. Once the craft table arrived, it beckoned me to write or do craft projects on the other side of the room. Eventually, some of my creations hung on the wall.

The Sustaining Power of Art

The studio inspired me to create, and it soon became my sanctuary. I'd work on charcoal drawings – mostly portraits – as well as write, make mosaics, refinish a piece of furniture, or scrapbook. I treasured moments to do something artistic while the kids were at school. At times, I would steal a few moments after school or on the weekends when Tonya or Lynn were there and try to drown out the demands for attention outside the door so I could recharge.

Art and music had always played such a huge part in my life that it felt good to reclaim my creativity.

Part of the reason art sustained me was because it was easier to stay in the moment as I practiced my creativity. As I focused on drawing the curvature of someone's lips, my intense focus drowned out other things that cried for my attention.

Lynn later explained the phenomenon to me as "mindfulness," which is the act of staying present in the moment and being fully aware of one's thoughts, feelings, bodily sensations, and surroundings, without judgment or feeling the need to act. As he explained it, I knew I needed to practice mindfulness more. It made me feel relaxed.

That January, I took an art class through the local Parks and Rec Department. Learning how to draw better allowed me to see immediate progress. As I put my charcoal pencil or pen to the paper, I could see the picture take form. If I missed a class, I could see it in my mood and my ability to handle the kids.

The studio also became the room where I started meeting with Jesus again. I spent mornings reading the Bible, praying, or worshiping with my guitar, with three dogs lying at my feet.

The studio restoration project did more than make the room beautiful. It restored my soul.

I had also begun to see how it contributed to restoring my family. My better mood, and the fact that Lynn and I were working more as a team, impacted the kids. The kids became more calm, which made our time with them much more enjoyable. Our family was healing.

Hiking with Michelle

By March, the weather was getting nice.

Michelle was a mom who attended our support group. She told me several times that my quest for health inspired her to practice better self-care. She was the best mom I knew at taking care of herself through exercise. Her regimen challenged me, because exercise was a struggle for me. We decided to hike Badger Mountain together.

"I've been reading this book on self-care," I mentioned to her as we walked up the hill, "and I'm learning a lot."

"Our society doesn't value self-care. We're taught to sacrifice and not to take care of ourselves at all."

"I agree. I wish it was different, though. I always feel guilty when I do something for myself."

"Me too. But our kids need to see us taking care of ourselves. It helps them learn that they can take care of themselves, too."

"What's the most significant thing *you* do for self-care?"

"I run, because running always makes me feel better." With a sly grin she added, "Of course, when I go for a run I always run faster when I'm going away from the kids and slower coming back home."

I laughed and then noticed how much work it was to keep up with her.

Must be because she runs all the time and I don't.

I felt energized after our walk, but a few hours later, I felt like I'd been run over by a Mac truck. I decided to make another appointment with Dr. Caporiccio to find out why.

Before my appointment, I tried a few more intense workouts but felt so wiped out afterwards that I stopped. I couldn't handle any kind of strenuous exercise without getting winded. Anytime I overdid it, I could barely get out of bed the next day. I frequently overestimated what I could do, now that I was feeling better.

A Visit to the Doctor

I once again sat in Dr. Caporiccio's office.

"I'm still not at 100 percent, but I'm feeling better," I told her. "I'm concerned about my energy levels, though. Every time I exercise, I immediately feel great but soon after, I feel like I've been run over by a bus."

"Remember how low your cortisol is during the day? Your adrenals are fatigued and struggling to keep up. You will need to stick to low-key exercise for a while to let them heal.

"Yoga or Pilates should work better, as long as it's nothing strenuous. Make sure you're eating small meals with protein throughout the day to prevent your blood sugar level from dropping. Your adrenals help stabilize blood sugar, so drops in blood sugar put extra strain on them."

It made sense. I'd heard the term "adrenal fatigue" before and made a mental note to look it up.

I mentioned gas, bloating, and other digestive issues I'd been having, and Dr. C decided to test for GI bacteria.

She handed me a box. "Here's a test kit. In the meantime, I'd like you to start on what I call a 'cleanse' diet. Here's an informational sheet, but basically, you will limit your diet to whole foods. Take out preservatives as much as possible and eat meats that are hormone-and-antibiotic free. Focus on eating fruits, veggies, nuts, and healthy fats, such as olive and coconut oils. As much as possible, I'd also like you to remove gluten, sugar, dairy, and soy from your diet because those foods create more stress on your system than other foods. The goal is to rid your body of toxins and provide the nutrients it needs."

My heart sank as she handed me the brochure. No junk food or lattes?

"I also want you to drink lots of water to flush out the toxins."

When I got home, I told Lynn about the diet.

"No sugar, no dairy, no gluten, no soy?" he challenged. "You mean no fun!"
"I'm not excited about it, but I'm willing to do anything to feel better."

After starting on the cleanse diet, I felt better than I had in years. The work it took to eat that way brought about a change of perspective for me. When making food choices, I asked myself, "Is it worth it? Will eating this nurture my body or bring in more toxins for me to have to get rid of later?"

I reminded myself that I was parenting on an Olympic level, and Olympians needed to care for their bodies to succeed. With high stress levels, I had to undo the negative impact by caring for my body at a much higher level than others did.

Ever since my first appointment with Dr. Caporiccio, Lynn had been making fun of me. "You're going to a quack," he'd say, laughing every time.

But after seeing how much better I'd been feeling, one day he sheepishly told me, "I made an appointment with your doctor."

New Foods

I set out on a mission to find new foods to eat that weren't boring or time con-suming. For the most part, searching for Paleo recipes worked best. I still liked to entertain my taste buds, but I had to keep in mind that the purpose of food came down to restoring and sustaining my body.

Dr. C's advice to eat frequently and include some sort of protein helped my ener-gy level tremendously, but despite drinking lots of water, I still felt dehydrated.

As I researched the adrenals, I discovered that besides producing cortisol, they also produce aldosterone, the hormone responsible for balancing water levels with electrolytes such as sodium and potassium. When the adrenals are not functioning well, they tend to flush out these electrolytes.

I noticed I often craved salty foods. I had always heard that salt intake should be limited, but I so strongly craved it that I started dumping sea salt or Himalayan salt on everything.

The next time I saw Dr. Caporiccio, I asked her about it. I expected her to yell at me, but she didn't.

"That makes sense. Your blood pressure has always been normal and even quite low at times, so you don't have to worry much about restricting your salt intake. As long as you're using Real Salt or Himalayan salt you should be fine, and we will monitor your sodium levels. I also recommend supplementing with an electrolyte tablet or powder in your water. By the way, have you sent in the GI test I gave you?"

She could tell by my look I hadn't. "Send it in."

After my appointment, I went to the supplement store and picked up several electrolyte drinks she recommended. I quickly noticed that when I used them in addition to the extra salt, they helped to alleviate much of my fatigue.

CHAPTER 20

I Want My Mommy

"Mom, I just don't know what's wrong with me," I started.

"What's going on?"

"I don't know. It's confusing. I'm crying at the drop of a hat and really irritable. I can't even stand to be in my own skin right now."

As I shared, it dawned on me that Mother's Day was approaching. I had begun to see a pattern in recent years. I began to feel depressed weeks before the holiday arrived. A growing sense of dread and tears would well up without warning. That day brought out such painful behavior in my children that I began to hate it.

Tears started streaming down my face. "I just want to get through the day, Mom. Other than giving *you* a gift and wishing *you* a Happy Mother's Day, I honestly would prefer to pretend it's a normal day or skip over it entirely. There's too much pain associated with this day, which is sad for me. I've dreamed of being a mom all my life."

"I wish I could reach through the phone and give you a big hug, Jennie. Until I can, take your right hand and put it on your left shoulder." She briefly paused.

"Now take your left hand and put it on your right shoulder... and squeeze," she said, repeating what she always said when I was homesick, starting when I went away to college.

I began to cry even more, wishing I could get a real hug from her. In that moment, I just wanted my mommy.

After I got off the phone, I remembered my expectations of what Mother's Day would look like before becoming a mother. Mother's Day used to conjure visions of plump little hands delivering carefully-colored cards, given with sloppy-wet kisses and big smiles. I pictured poorly-wrapped presents they would have made for me at school. They would giggle over my obvious excitement, throw in a hearty "I love you Mommy!" then run off and play while my husband treated me like a queen.

The reality was quite different. Lynn and I took Bri and Stephen camping for my first Mother's Day. They were not fun to be around, as Mother's Day was a trigger for them.

My second Mother's Day was about six months after Parker came to live with us. After making a clay creation in class meant to be a present for his mom, he asked his teacher what he should do with it.

"Well... uh... ummm," she sputtered, surprised at his question, "why not give it to your adoptive mom?"

Instead he broke it. Then he gave it to me in five pieces, six weeks after Mother's Day.

Lynn worked hard to make Mother's Day beautiful. He took the kids out to shop for a gift, sometimes even picking out the gift from Parker so that he couldn't sabotage it. He would wake them early and help them make breakfast in bed for me. He had the kids pick out cards and tried to get them excited to show me gratitude. Lynn also always purchased a larger gift from him, such as a nice spa package or lawn furniture.

Bri and Stephen, after years of hard work and lots of healing, started to anticipate the arrival of Mother's Day and got excited about planning gifts on their own.

On a good year with Parker, Mother's Day consisted of me comforting him because he missed the other moms in his life and wanted to be with them instead of me. Even when he was doing much better, he would engage in subtle jabs, putting his name on the envelope rather than mine, or writing a rude comment on the card.

Mother's Day also served as a reminder to me of deep, personal losses. The title "mom" was never exclusively for me. My child's birth mom got the privilege of carrying them in her womb. She got to see the first sonogram and hear that sweet baby's first cry. She got to snuggle with a precious newborn and drink in the smell of her baby's freshly-washed head. She, or one of the others privileged to be called "mom" along the way, observed my child's first steps and witnessed them lose their first tooth.

I didn't even have baby pictures.

Mother's Day was a reminder that I would never be the first mom in my kids' hearts, even after they healed and bonded with me. Especially in the beginning, they loved another mom much more than they loved me. Even though I expected that, it didn't make the loss less painful. I wasn't the mom they wanted to be with, and they made that clear in the early years.

Mother's Day became a reminder of the years I had missed. I didn't get to know my children before the damage had been done. I felt sad about never being able to play "patty cake" with them. By the time they lived with me, they were too old for nursery rhymes. I missed picking out adorable little baby outfits for them, sitting on the floor playing blocks, and teaching them how to ride a bike. I also wasn't there to protect them, which I would have loved to do.

Adventure with Stephen

"I feel bad saying it, but I would love to go somewhere with just Stephen," I told Lynn as I petted Sport, who was resting on my lap. "He's the only one who is fun to be around right now. I feel like I neglect him because the other two take so much energy."

"Why don't you?"

"I don't want the other two to feel left out."

"You've been wanting to go to Wisconsin to see your parents; why don't you take him with you?"

"That sounds like a BLAST, but what will we do with the other two?"

"The director of Camp Spalding has been trying to get me out to see their summer camp, and we're sending a group of kids from church in June. I'll go with the group myself and take Parker with me."

"What about Bri?"

"Maybe my mom can take her for the week. That way, each kid has an adult spending one-on-one time with them. We get a break from her attitude, and she gets fun time with Grandma."

"I love it! You talk to your mom, and I'll buy plane tickets for Stephen and me."

A month later, Stephen and I were on the plane to Wisconsin. We arrived at the Atlanta airport late when our connection from Phoenix was delayed. We missed the flight to Milwaukee and found out we would have to take an early morning flight. It was already 12:30 a.m. and our flight left at 5:00 a.m., so it hardly seemed worth finding a hotel and going back through security.

"What do you think about hanging out in the airport until our flight? We could have our own little adventure," I asked.

"Sure! I like adventure!"

I smiled at his enthusiasm.

"OK, adventure it is."

It seemed like an adventure until the security guard kicked us out of the secured part of the airport around 2:00 a.m.

"Why don't we hang out by those chairs over there?" I said to Stephen. It was carpeted, and though it was accessible from the street, we weren't outside. Hanging with the homeless didn't seem as much fun as staying in the airport terminal, but by then it seemed really silly to get a hotel room.

"I think I'm going to lie on the floor for a while, Stephen."

"Me too," he said, as he laid his head on my stomach.

We'd been there about two minutes when I started to feel like a thousand, tiny bugs were biting my flesh.

"OUCH! Do you feel that?" I said as I sat up.

"I feel all itchy."

"Yes, it feels like I'm being bitten, too."

"Me, too!"

"Well, looks like we are DEFINITELY having an adventure. I guess we'll just have to try to get comfortable in these chairs."

Stephen lay rolled up in the chair next to me, his head on my lap.

At least one of us will get some sleep.

Around 4:00 a.m., he stirred.

"Buddy, we should head over and go back into the airport now. The Starbucks over there is open. Do you want to get something for breakfast?"

"It's part of our adventure!"

"Yep."

We stood at the counter. "Can I have a muffin?" he asked.

"Yes, and would you like some coffee?" I never let the kids have coffee, and I knew he'd be excited.

"YES!! Oh, this *is* a fun adventure, Mom!" he said, jumping up and down. "Can I buy this mug with my own money, too? I want to remember this!"

"Of course."

My brother picked up our tired bodies at the Milwaukee airport later that morning.

After telling the story of our adventure in the Atlanta airport, we slept for a couple of hours before my parents arrived. By then, we both got our second wind, so we retold the story of being kicked out of the secured part of the airport, including our little bug invasion and trying to sleep on the chairs.

That week, Mom taught Stephen how to sew. She'd shown him a new toy in the store called "Ugly Dolls" and got him excited about making a monster of his own. I enjoyed seeing how proud he was of his finished product.

Stephen and I watched orioles eat the grape jelly my parents left out for them. I loved listening to the sound of birds chirping and the wind rustling through the trees. At our own home, we had tried to work on landscaping, but there was too much work needed to make the yard a relaxing place. Just being there, spending time with my parents in the quiet of the country, I felt my soul restored.

"Whatever happened with the GI test you were supposed to take?" my mom asked as we sat and talked. "Did you ever get the results?"

"I haven't even taken it yet."

"Jennie, it's been four months since she told you to take that test. Go get it done," she said, emphatically.

"OK."

"If Grandma or Aunt Lisa Were My Mom..."

When we got back home, I took the test Dr. Caporiccio recommended and thought about how nice it had been to spend time with Stephen. I enjoyed being around him, and it was nice knowing I'd caught up a bit on giving him the much-needed attention he deserved, but rarely got.

Brianna was meaner to me than she had been before I left. I soon realized she'd been up to her usual "mommy shopping" with Grandma and Aunt Lisa. It seemed that any amount of fun with any woman besides me precipitated more mommy shopping. After about a week of increasingly rude behavior, I said to her, "Bri, I think you may be confused about what life would be like if you lived with Grandma or Aunt Lisa."

"Mom, if Grandma or Aunt Lisa were my mom THEY wouldn't make me do my chores," she said in a huff, with an attitude bigger than the state of Texas.

"Sweetheart, I hate to break it to you, but you'd have to do some sort of chore in ANY family you joined."

"No, Mom. THEY wouldn't make me do CHORES OR clean my room. I bet *they'd* give me more attention than *YOU* do! AND more candy! I bet they'd even take me shopping more!"

They hadn't given her one piece of candy or taken her shopping the entire week, so I highly doubted the last part. But frequently her fantasies didn't line up with reality.

I remembered her mommy shopping incident the Christmas right after we moved. She'd gone with a friend and her friend's mom on two separate days to do something fun. When she returned the second time, she wailed for two hours, her body heaving, before I was able to calm her down. After she started to calm down, I realized what was going on.

"Brianna, finish this sentence for me: If she were my mom..."

Through the sobs she answered, "... she ... she ... pht ... would ... pht ... pht ... take ... me ... pht ... shopping... EVERY SINGLE DAY!"

"Sweetheart, I know you think she would take you shopping every day, but you only spent two days with her. I doubt that she goes shopping every day. It's two weeks before Christmas, and EVERYBODY goes shopping this time of year."

"No, Mom. *Every* time I hung out with them she took us shopping. She would take me shopping EVERY day if she was my mom! I just KNOW it!" Though she had finally calmed down, she realized what she had just said and began to cry again.

I tried to reason with her, but despite my attempts to help her understand reality, she insisted that this woman, with whom she had spent less than two days, would take her shopping every day if she was her mom. She was convinced of it.

Realizing that I was getting nowhere, I said, "Well even if she WOULD take you every day to the mall, it doesn't matter. *I'M* your mom, and *that's* not going to change. Like it or not, you're stuck with me forever."

Hoping others could help her understand, I mentioned the situation to Sharon and Lisa.

"Well, she would *definitely* have to do chores if she lived with me!" Sharon said, "All of my kids did chores!"

"She wouldn't want to live with me either, then," added Lisa, "because I'd make her do chores."

"I know, but she doesn't believe me when I tell her that," I said. "Could you guys explain that to her?"

"Why don't you have her come over tomorrow, and we will spend some time with her," Sharon said, and Lisa nodded.

After they set Brianna straight about her fantasies and reinforced that she already had a good mom who loved her, Bri came back a much happier, healthier kiddo.

I was so thankful for the way they and others, like Heidi, the Nursery Coordinator at church, and Jenny, another good friend, supported us and encouraged Brianna in her relationship with us.

Stress and the Gut

The next month, Dr. Caporiccio's office called to set up an appointment for her to go over the test results with me.

"Your intestines have pretty much been taken over by yeast and unhealthy bacteria," Dr. Caporiccio said. "You have SIBO, or Small Intestinal Bacterial Overgrowth, and a yeast overgrowth. Candida, the yeast, feeds off sugar, so it's very important that you stay on the diet I gave you earlier. I'm going to give you some supplements to help kill it. You also have very little good bacteria in your system, so I'm going to put you on a strong probiotic to raise that number."

"How did all this happen?"

"Stress can certainly do this. I work with several families who've adopted challenging children, and a lot of them deal with the same types of issues."

When I left her office, I did more research.

The human brain can't distinguish between being chased by a hungry lion and dealing with a ten-year-old throwing a tantrum. When it perceives any threat, blood pressure increases, the heart pumps more quickly, and the blood vessels narrow to more quickly send blood to the larger muscle groups. Blood is diverted away from some internal organs, and we go into "fight, flight, or freeze" mode.

When blood bypasses our digestive system, it doesn't receive the nutrients necessary to sustain healthy flora. This allows unhealthy bacteria and yeast to take over the GI tract.

The GI system is often called the "second brain," due to the more than thirty neurotransmitters located there, so this also negatively impacts our mood.

Each stressful encounter with my children caused my body to release extra stress hormones, which – in turn – caused a lot of troublesome physical conditions.

CHAPTER 21

Beyond Mom

That fall, Brianna was going into seventh grade; Stephen was in fifth grade, and Parker was starting middle school.

"You need to get a job," the kids' therapist said, looking at me sternly.

"I've already got my hands full with the kids. Why would you tell me to get a job?"

"Well, for one thing, your health is improving and you're feeling better, right?"

She was right. As soon as I'd started taking the protocol for SIBO the doctor had put me on, my energy increased, and I was quickly shedding pounds. I was buying jeans at Goodwill until my weight loss slowed, because I would buy a new pair of jeans and within weeks they were too big for me.

I was feeling much better — but a job?

"Yes, but..."

Before I could say more, she continued, "You need another focus besides the kids. You need an outlet that gets you out into the world and keeps your mind off them."

My life did seem to center on them and their issues. I knew that wasn't healthy, and if it wasn't healthy for me, it wasn't good for any of us.

I wasn't thrilled about the idea, but I began to understand that my life needed to stop revolving around my children. My entire identity was invested in being a mom.

"I'll consider it, but right now I want to talk about Parker's booger wiping issue. Nothing we've done has stopped it, and I am tired of finding boogers everywhere."

"All right. But you have to promise you'll at least think about getting a job."

The therapist sat quietly for a moment, deep in thought. Her eyes lit up. "Well, you've tried to get him to stop this game. Maybe you need to play it with him."

"That's disgusting! Are you serious?"

"Why not? We've tried everything else, and nothing has worked. He obviously doesn't want to stop. This way you can connect with him at the same time."

The idea grossed me out, but the next day after school, I met him at the door.

"You know, Parker, I've been going about this all wrong. I am so sorry. All this time I've been trying to get you to stop leaving boogers all over the house, but you really like this game.

"Personally, I'd prefer to play Monopoly with you, but since I love you so much and you like to play this booger game, I've decided to play too. I've placed several of my own boogers in your bedroom, so you can play the game of finding them."

My statement made Parker visibly angry, but I rarely found boogers after that.

The "Luxury" of Self-Care

That November, we were again asked to speak at the Heart for the Fatherless Conference. As the conference neared, I got excited. I had learned so much that I was glad to have the chance to share.

I was still tired and in the middle of the struggle, but I knew other moms needed to hear what I had learned.

I presented a workshop on discipline to a full crowd, challenging parents to practice self-care in order to discipline well. As I briefly shared some of the normal emotions I had experienced while parenting challenging kids, I noticed a woman in the audience whose sobs could be heard from the front of the large room. There were several others tearing up. I had hit a nerve.

Lynn later spoke about the impact of trauma on the brain, then taught a class on attachment. Both of his classes also gathered full crowds.

I was disappointed in the attendance at my last class, "How to Practice Good Self-Care While Parenting Wounded Kids." Only six people came, two of whom were good friends offering support. Most of the parents of traumatized children were operating like I had been. They were in survival mode, just trying to make it through the day. Self-care seemed like a luxury to them.

Go Easy On Yourself

Earlier that November, the middle school director at our church quit. Lynn tried to convince me to consider taking the job.

"It would be perfect for you with your youth ministry experience, and we can make it part-time. There's a young guy who could do a lot of the speaking. You wouldn't have to come up with all the messages."

"I don't know, Lynn," I said at first.

I loved mentoring teenagers, planning events, and leading teams. While this was a more demanding job than the kids' therapist had in mind, I remembered her suggestion. The thought of working in youth ministry again excited me.

Both Brianna and Parker were in middle school now. Most of the time I could work while the kids were in school. If I were leading the church's middle school program, I could keep tabs on them, and Lynn and I would feel better about having them attend youth group. We hadn't yet felt comfortable with having them go.

I ended up taking the job and quickly loved what I was doing.

A couple of months later, I was talking with Delores, the church bookkeeper. She had quickly become a dear friend.

"I feel bad, Delores. I feel like I've been using this job to avoid my kids." I half expected a look of disapproval or a judgmental comment.

Her look of compassion encouraged me. "It's not that I don't love them; it's just that the kids in the middle school program actually like me and don't do mean things to me. The kids here are restoring my faith in humanity. It feels good to be appreciated and treated kindly. This job has given me its share of challenges, but the kudos outweigh the difficulties. I have been so tempted with my kids to phone it in, especially since in many ways they're doing better."

"I don't know how you've done it, Jennie. Most people wouldn't be able to handle one deeply wounded child. You have THREE! You need to go easier on yourself."

Her kind words elicited a free flow of tears.

"You've done everything God has asked you to do. Have you done it perfectly? No. But He knows you are weary. He even knows you have, at times, used work to avoid your children, but you may have also used it as a means of survival."

She was right. I did need to go easier on myself.

Given the difficulty of parenting my children, I would never have criticized others as harshly as I was criticizing myself. I was expecting perfection, not allowing myself to just be or offering myself any compassion.

I was beating myself up over shoulds and should nots.

"I should be able to handle this better."

"I shouldn't let this bother me."

"I should be doing more to help my children heal."

I even judged myself for not practicing better self-care.

Her words challenged me to be more compassionate with myself. I even found a few quotes to remind me to do so. Gradually, as I had more compassion for myself, I was able to offer my children more as well.

> *You can have compassion for yourself—which is not self-pity.*
> *You're simply recognizing that "this is tough, this hurts," and*
> *bringing the same warmhearted wish for suffering to lessen or end*
> *that you would bring to any dear friend grappling with the same*
> *pain, upset, or challenges as you.*
>
> *– Rick Hanson, Just One Thing*

Oxygen Mask

That winter, I found that having a job was helping me with the kids. Because I had something outside of their issues to occupy my mind, I was able to respond to their poor choices in a calmer manner.

In early spring, I could tell I needed another big break from the kids.

"I'm about to lose it. I have to get away for awhile," I told Lynn.

"You should visit your parents."

"That's exactly what I was thinking. My mom's birthday is coming up, and I'd like to surprise her. Especially since my Aunt Anna's funeral, I feel the need to be around family."

Three weeks later, I boarded the plane and took my seat.

The flight attendant began her instructions. As I watched her bring the oxygen mask toward her face, a phrase stuck out to me in a way it never had before.

"If you are traveling with a child or someone who requires assistance, secure your mask first and then assist the other person."

How had I heard this so many times and never made the connection between this advice and a wonderful life lesson? Many of the struggles I experienced over the past few years had been because I'd been putting my kids' oxygen masks on before my own.

While I'd gotten better at practicing self-care, I still felt guilty every time I did something for myself. But just like on the airplane, parents aren't any good to their children if they've passed out or died due to lack of oxygen.

I pondered the idea for a while and then took a short nap.

As the plane descended, I teared up, knowing that for the next few days I wouldn't have to be strong anymore.

Any time I let my guard down, tears came. In order to survive, I had stuffed my emotions so deeply that when I allowed myself to relax, they quickly came to the surface.

Just breathe, I told myself. I forced the tears back into their cage so the flight attendants wouldn't find a blubbering mess on the floor near seat 16C, with the other passengers impatiently stepping over my heaving body.

As much as I tried to keep my tears at bay, they came streaming down the second I saw my dad. He came to pick me up alone so we could surprise my mom. I hugged him, he grabbed my bag, and we headed off to the car. We chatted on the short ride home about the party we planned for Mom.

I walked in the door of my parents' house, and my mom squealed with glee. I hugged her tight. It was so good to be where I was well-known and well-loved. For a short time, I could just be taken care of.

I was tired from the trip, so I retired early that night after I took a bath. Dad told me about putting a cup of pure hydrogen peroxide and a cup and a half of magnesium flakes in hot bath water and soaking in it for a while. I sweated like a pig but fell asleep quickly and slept better than I had in a long time.

Over the next few days, I spent time chatting with my parents and watching birds stop by their backyard feeders for a snack. Behind them, I could see horses from the neighbor's property gracefully eating hay, with the steeple of a picturesque country church in the distance. I felt restored.

Goodbye to Captain

It wasn't until May of that year that I realized how far Parker had come.

We were sitting around the living room watching TV when Captain started heaving and struggling to breathe. Lynn and I knew that he was close to the end of his life and considered having him put down. We just hadn't been able to bring ourselves to do so. As it became clear that he wasn't doing well, we loaded him and all the kids in the van, leaving the little dogs in the backyard.

Lynn sat in the back of the van, trying to comfort Captain, and I drove, tears flowing down my face, to the closest animal hospital. I heard a chorus of sobs behind me. I looked back and saw the kids, even Parker, openly weeping. I couldn't help but notice the pain in Parker's face over Captain's suffering.

What a difference from two years ago when I took all three dogs to the vet. The vet took Sport back to another room to discharge the buildup in his anal sac, and Sport yelped loudly. Bri, Stephen, and I moaned as we thought of the poor little dog in pain. As I looked over at Parker he was grinning from ear to ear, enjoying Sport's pain.

I thought about the many times he had tried to hurt the animals, with little emotional connection to what he was doing. I was amazed at the empathy I now saw in him. Parker had developed a conscience.

I had never understood so clearly how connected conscience development was to a child's attachments. I'd read that children develop a conscience as they are able to trust the adults in their lives, but this made it much more obvious.

I had always been bothered by the way my kids could hurt others and not seem to care. I secretly thought it made them bad kids. But there's no way they could have had a conscience until they started to trust.

They'd made so much progress without my noticing.

On the way to the animal hospital, Lynn gave the kids some time with Captain. Both Parker and Stephen said goodbye. When we arrived, Lynn ran to get help, and I caught up with Brianna.

"I noticed you didn't say goodbye to Captain."

"I just can't, Mom." Tears ran down her face.

"Honey, I think if you don't say goodbye, you're going to regret it."

We walked together to the back of the van where Captain lay. I stood next to her with my hand on her back as she placed her hand on his head. Captain let out a big sigh and was gone.

"I think he was waiting to say goodbye to you before he left," I told her. Brianna nodded.

Lynn was back with a vet tech. They lifted Captain's body onto the rolling table and wheeled him back.

"He's already gone, Lynn," I told him.

The veterinarian led us into a room and asked if we wanted to see Captain one more time. We each petted his already stiffening body and said our last goodbyes.

As we left, I asked Brianna, "Are you glad you said goodbye to him before he died?"

"Yes." Her swollen eyes brightened.

Captain had been Brianna's buddy ever since she was at Place of Hope. She would lie on his belly as she watched TV and snuggle with him at every opportunity. She loved that dog, and he loved her.

From the day Brianna entered our home, she loved animals. She was mean to people but loving to animals, and even the skittish ones flocked to her. When we watched a movie, twenty people could be shot and she would say nothing. As soon as a dog or horse would die, she'd cry.

Later, as she healed, children flocked to her as well.

It was good to see my children healing.

Chapter 22

Compassion Fatigue

The lack of services for foster and adoptive families in our area inspired Lynn to go back to school to become a licensed mental health counselor.

At the end of the summer, I joined him in Virginia for his last week of on-site schooling. He attended classes during the day while I hung out at Virginia Beach. One night at dinner, Lynn said, "I heard the term 'compassion fatigue' in class and was thinking it's something that moms of traumatized kids experience."

"Just hearing the term makes a lot of sense to me. It's as if you get tired of showing compassion."

The next day, I visited the library and researched the term.

I discovered that counselors, doctors, nurses, and others who interact with traumatized people are the ones who typically suffer from compassion fatigue. While not a formal diagnosis in the DSM (Diagnostic and Statistical Manual of Mental Disorders), compassion fatigue describes helpers who experience isolation, apathy, sadness, fatigue, and other symptoms from being immersed in trauma without adequate self-care. Some use the term interchangeably with burnout, vicarious traumatization, or secondary traumatic stress.

I began to think of compassion as a muscle or organ, just like the heart or a leg muscle, or even the adrenal glands. Giving compassion in healthy balance is good, but overusing the "muscle" without enough rest causes problems.

The more I researched, the more my experience made sense. I had already realized that while I was walking beside my children in their trauma and pain, it had slowly become my own. Knowing the soul-crushing events that had occurred in my children's lives cut deeply. Exponentially more heartbreaking was watching them repeatedly make harmful choices, knowing that I couldn't control their decisions. At times, the sorrow and heartbreak were unbearable.

Understanding compassion fatigue meant knowing I wasn't a bad person for feeling so jaded, cynical, and uncaring. A few months earlier, I'd read a post from another adoptive mom and connected with what she said: "Sometimes parenting wounded children is a repeated process of having your heart ripped apart a little at a time until you are very cynical."

I had reached the point of cynicism too, and I felt like I'd become a monster. I felt terrible as I found it difficult to handle my children's big emotions or to be there for a struggling friend.

Later, I read a statement by Rachel Remen, MD, that helped make sense of it. "The expectation that we can be immersed in suffering and loss daily and not be touched by it is as unrealistic as expecting to be able to walk through water without getting wet."

Brianna and Stephen's Birth Mom Dies

The fall that Brianna started high school, we got a call from Cindy, the kids' former therapist from Florida. Brianna and Stephen's birth mother had surgery to remove a brain tumor, and it didn't look like she would live long. We packed up and flew to Florida to give the kids a chance to say goodbye.

At the hospital, we told the staff who we were and explained that the kids wanted to see their mom. A nurse pulled Lynn and me aside.

"You need to know that we don't normally allow children in this ward, but given your situation, we are willing to make an exception. You need to understand that it's bad. She had a brain tumor removed. Her head is shaved. She has tubes in her head to keep the fluids drained. It might scare the kids. If you, as the parents, say it's OK, we will allow this visit, but you need to know that it may be tough for them to see her like this."

"They need to see her," Lynn told her. "We will help them process what they see."

As we walked into the room, the tubes coming out of her head made her look more like a cyborg than the beautiful woman she was. I noted her shaved head and felt an overwhelming sadness.

Brianna and Stephen's mom had always been a drop-dead gorgeous woman. Long, flowing hair, a bright smile, and high cheek bones made her look like a model. I had noticed how her life choices had stolen some of that beauty, but the surgery seemed to take away even her humanity.

I was sad when I thought of all this woman had missed. I looked at her two beautiful children and felt sad that drugs caused them all to miss years of relationship well before we came into the picture. I watched Brianna and Stephen's solemn faces as they held her hand, searching for the mom they remembered.

Minutes later, anger joined the wide range of emotions swirling inside my heart. The woman lying there had made choices that forever impacted my little ones and had made my life more challenging.

Cindy had once told me that she would check in with the birth mom from time to time to make sure she was doing well. She had worked with the biological family for more than two years and truly cared for them. She wanted to make sure their mom knew she was still loved, even though Brianna and Stephen no longer lived with her.

During these visits, their mom would weep as she brought out the kids' pictures. She explained that she couldn't keep their pictures out because the pain of losing them was too deep to bear. As she sat with Cindy, she would look at their faces and weep even more bitterly.

It was easier for me to justify my anger when I thought of her as a monster who chose drugs over her kids. Deep down, I knew she loved Brianna and Stephen. But she had been barely able to care for herself. How could she take care of them? That's what I always told the kids.

Watching her lying there, lifeless, I thought about what Cindy had told me, and the anger turned into pity. Being apart from her children could not have been easy.

We spent a few days with the kids' extended family, including their older brother and several of their mom's friends. It was a struggle to be around so many people whose values differed from ours, but the upside was hearing stories about their childhood and being allowed to go through family photos. We bought a scanner and scanned as many pictures as we could. I was thankful to finally have pictures of them when they were young, but it saddened me to still not have any of Parker.

Disney Meltdown

To give ourselves a break, we took the kids to Disney World. We spent time in Downtown Disney the first night, checking out the stores and performances. We spent a little time listening to a musical performance before deciding to go to the next store.

Parker wanted to stay and listen to the next song. He was now fifteen years old and had been doing much better, so we pointed to the store across the street and told him to meet us there. We kept an eye out for him, checking every few minutes while we were in the store.

About ten minutes later, I saw him come to the front of the building, so I went out to meet him. Looking right at me, he proceeded to walk past me multiple times, much like he'd done years earlier when I picked him up from middle school.

When the family gathered to go to the next store, we flagged him down, but not before he had a major meltdown.

"YOU GUYS LEFT ME!" he yelled at Lynn.

"Parker, we were right there in the store. You walked right past us multiple times," Lynn countered as he walked toward the next store.

"Parker, he's right. You kept walking right past us." I added, "You looked right at me and kept going."

Parker ignored my comment and ran toward Lynn in hot pursuit, his arms flailing as he screamed, "You BASTARD! You weren't where you said you would be, and you left me!"

I was thankful that we'd walked to where there were fewer people to give us funny looks. I was also a bit relieved that he was screaming at Lynn for a change. Lynn tried reasoning with him once more and then walked, knowing that nothing he could say would calm Parker. Parker followed him, screaming even louder, "YOU F***! YOU ABANDONED ME!"

I followed behind Lynn, keeping an eye on Parker, unsure of what he would do. I looked over at Brianna and Stephen and saw stress on their faces. Lynn walked for a while, turned in to a secluded place and stopped, calmly sitting on a nearby bench. Parker joined him on the bench, and I stood a little way off, near Lynn and Parker in case Lynn needed help — but far enough away to feel safe.

I turned to Brianna and Stephen. "Why don't you guys go to the next store without us." As they gladly walked away, my heart wouldn't stop racing. Eventually, Parker calmed down, and we finished walking around Downtown Disney. Despite my determination to not let it affect me, his outburst took the fun out of the evening. His meltdowns, though they were now rarer, quickly depleted my resources.

We spent two days at Disney World before returning to the hospital, where Brianna and Stephen said their tearful last goodbyes to their mom, and we headed for home.

CHAPTER 23

Post-Traumatic Stress Disorder

I was standing in the laundry room a week later when I stopped breathing and became very tense. My heart raced.

As I tried to process what had happened, it dawned on me. We had just dropped Parker off at a friend's house. Had he been with us, it would have been about five minutes after our return home that he would start questioning me or want something from me.

I began to notice my body reacting almost every time Parker walked into the room. My blood pressure would immediately rise, and my jaws would clench. I would hold my breath in anticipation of the negative interaction that would likely come along with him. His behavior was improving, but I would startle or overreact, as if automatically responding to an old situation.

"It sounds like a PTSD response," Ryan, Lynn's counseling practice partner, said.

"The counselor I went to a while back told me I have PTSD. I feel like I need to have my guard up with him."

"Don't feel badly, Jennie. I think Parker's presence is a trauma trigger for you."

As we talked, I realized how much PTSD had affected me. When the other counselor mentioned it, I dismissed its impact on my daily life. I also allowed others to deny or invalidate what I was experiencing.

"You don't have PTSD," one person said. "You have to have been in physical danger to have that."

When I explained it to Ryan, he shook his head. "Actually, that's not true. Look at the DSM-V," he said as he pulled out the diagnostic manual used by counselors. "It says PTSD can come from personally experiencing trauma or from someone close to you experiencing traumatic events. You had both."

"Really? I was told if it's from someone else's trauma it's called 'Secondary PTSD.'"

"No. It says here that experiencing secondary trauma is included in the criteria for being diagnosed with PTSD."

"That makes me mad. Do you know how many adoptive and foster moms out there are experiencing PTSD and people are telling them it's just their imagination? Secondary trauma is real. It *IS* traumatizing to hear about the terrible abuse a child has gone through."

"On top of that, you experienced a lot of trauma from what the kids did *to* you," he reminded me, "Remember there was a time when you feared for your safety with Parker."

"That's true. I started seeing the world as an unsafe place. It felt pretty scary to me."

He continued to read. "Criterion C: Avoidance: Persistent effortful avoidance of distressing trauma-related stimuli after the event, either (1) Trauma-related thoughts or feelings, or (2) Trauma-related external reminders (e.g., people, places, conversations, activities, objects, or situations)."

After reading the criteria for me, he looked up and said, "I think that fits. It makes sense that you'd want to avoid your kids. It's not that you're a bad mom, as you seem to believe. It's because they, themselves, are reminders of the trauma you went through with them. It's not like you're *trying* to feel that way about them. It is what it is. It's where you are. Keep in mind that PTSD symptoms can come up years after the trauma occurs."

The more Ryan talked, the more things clicked. I was still having trauma responses. It made a lot of sense that a challenging child or their specific behaviors could become a PTSD trigger, much like a car backfiring or fireworks can trigger a trauma response in a combat soldier. Like that soldier's brain, my brain automatically went back to experiences of old trauma when Parker walked into a room or when he started to have a meltdown, even though he had improved.

"That makes so much sense. And you know, I think it's common for parents of special needs kids or kids who have been through trauma. I see the same types of responses from other parents. Just like mine, most of their homes have become more like war zones than places of safety, especially those whose kids are violent toward them. I have a lot of friends who have gone through that."

Deep Breathing

Over the years, I noticed my PTSD symptoms came out more as the kids healed. At first it confused me, but I realized that it was happening as I felt safer. Although we were all doing better, I still felt like a soldier, grenades going off around me. Long after their behaviors drastically changed, all it took was a glimpse of an old pattern to send me right back to the time when parenting was like hell on earth.

The more I understood the trauma of what I had endured over the past few years, the more I was able to show compassion for myself. Just as my children's trauma had affected them and their behavior toward me, the trauma I endured had affected my response to them.

As I learned more about PTSD and trauma, I began to discover the importance of deep breathing. I learned that breathing is one of the few bodily functions under both conscious and autonomic control. When we are relaxed, our breathing vastly differs from when we are stressed. While relaxed, we breathe deeply and slowly, allowing air to fill our entire lungs before exhaling, which reduces muscle tension.

Conversely, holding our breath or taking fast, shallow breaths becomes a signal to the body that we are in danger, increasing the heart rate and blood pressure and setting in motion a "fight, flight or freeze" response.

I learned that people who hold their breath or have an elevated respiratory rate during a traumatic event are 1.79 times more likely to develop PTSD than those who maintain slower breathing during the event.

I decided to start breathing deeply, even though I'd grown so used to shallow breathing that it hurt to force that much air into my lungs. At first it was hard, but it became possible with correct practice.

Practicing deep breathing helped me feel more relaxed overall and helped relieve fatigue and depression. Stressful situations would arise, and I would have to remind myself to breathe, but as I practiced during non-stressful times, it got easier.

A few weeks after we returned from Florida, Brianna and Stephen's mom died. We couldn't afford to fly back for the funeral, so we invited friends and family over for a memorial service. We planted a tree in our front yard in her honor with a small marker on the ground beside it.

Bri struggled with her birth mother's death.

At the next therapy session, she insinuated she wished I had been the one to die instead. I'd grown used to comments like that and knew she was struggling and didn't mean it.

A week or so later, Brianna posted sweet notes around my office at the church. Several co-workers looked with confusion at the note that read, "I'm glad you're not dead."

The Mind-Body Connection

As I began to process the trauma from parenting wounded children, I found there was still something missing from my healing journey. I couldn't put my finger on it, but it was almost as if the trauma was stuck in my body. It felt like an unwanted prisoner, something I didn't want to hold on to, but I didn't know how to let go. No amount of verbal or written processing was helping.

"Maybe it's a matter of forgiveness," Lynn said one day. "Maybe you are still holding on to some bitterness toward the kids. At times when I watch you with them, you seem like you don't like them."

I thought about one time that I was getting a massage. As soon as the massage therapist touched me, I sobbed uncontrollably. It was as if the muscle she was working on had released pent-up emotions.

"I don't think that's it. I think it goes back to trauma, rather than forgiveness. It's almost as if I can feel it in different parts of my body. I'm beginning to believe there's a huge mind-body connection when it comes to trauma."

I found a book, *The Body Keeps the Score: Brain, Mind, and Body in the Healing of Trauma* by Bessel van der Kolk, MD. He explained that trauma is stored in a different part of the brain than language, which makes it hard to connect to or talk about it. He said that people with PTSD are on constant sensory overload and that "all trauma is preverbal."

After reading that book, I decided to go to a chiropractor that a friend had recommended. She had encouraged me to go for a long time, but I had resisted. Lately, I had seen significant changes in her mood, so I decided to give it a try. It certainly couldn't hurt.

Dr. Kris practiced something called NET or Neuro Emotional Technique. I didn't always fully understand what happened, but I often walked away from a session with a new perspective. Whatever he did connected to old trauma in a way that multiple counseling sessions never could.

I tried to find someone local who practiced Somatic Experiencing, a modality that van der Kolk recommended, but couldn't find one. I looked for a counselor who specialized in EMDR (Eye Movement Desensitization and Reprocessing) therapy, because my research suggested that it could also be helpful for PTSD. This technique connected to the trauma that seemed to be held deep inside my body.

I ended up figuring out that a weighted blanket also helped release trauma from my body.

I had always thought of weighted blankets as being strictly for people with autism or sensory issues, but they were being sold at a conference I attended for foster and adoptive parents. The vendor encouraged me to lie down in their reclining chair, so I reluctantly tried it.

After sitting there for less than ten minutes, I experienced a huge release of emotion and felt my body relax. When I got up, I felt like I'd taken a long nap. Both Lynn and I ended up getting one, and they helped us so much physically and emotionally that neither of us went on an overnight trip without them.

Neurotransmitters

It took awhile, but that fall my nighttime cortisol was within normal levels.

Dr. Caporiccio turned her attention to increasing my cortisol levels during the day. This first approach ended up not working as well as she had hoped.

"I have another idea I'd like to try," she said at another appointment. "Here's a kit to test your neurotransmitters."

I didn't even know what neurotransmitters were. Later I looked up the definition: "Neurotransmitter: any of several chemical substances, as epinephrine or acetylcholine, that transmit nerve impulses across a synapse to a postsynaptic element, as another nerve, muscle, or gland."

It still didn't make sense.

As Dr. Caporiccio went over the results later, things became clearer.

"OK, see this neurotransmitter listed here? GABA is supposed to calm you down. Yours is low, so that's going to cause sleep difficulties and anxiety.

"These neurotransmitters are meant to give you energy. Your norepinephrine is low, which can cause fatigue, low mood, and weight issues, as well as the focus and memory issues you've been having." I'd gained back quite a bit of weight since I hadn't been focusing as much on taking good care of myself. I was also still struggling with depression, despite taking antidepressants.

"Glutamate, PEA, and epinephrine also get you going, but yours are too high, so that can cause anxiety, focus issues, and sleep difficulties. The high PEA can cause your mind to race, which contributes to sleep problems."

The test results made perfect sense. Stress had caused my body to get out of whack, and I was excited to find something that could possibly help.

The test came back with a recommended list of supplements, which Dr. Caporiccio had already ordered. As she handed them to me, she gave me the "mom" look. "This doesn't replace the need to rest and take good care of yourself." She knew that while I had come a long way, my natural tendency was to push myself way too hard.

Taking these supplements helped my fatigue like nothing else we had tried. Resting and taking things off my stress load also helped. I was working with Vicki, the dietitian on Dr. Caporiccio's staff, who had a son with autism and understood my levels of stress. She recommended that I take extra magnesium, vitamin C, and B-vitamins, since those vitamins are quickly spent during times of stress.

The extra supplements helped tremendously. For a year and a half, I'd had an eye twitch that wouldn't go away. I laughed at the thought that for a long time I probably looked like I was winking at everybody. I'd also felt nervous, like I was about to speak to a huge crowd of people.

After increasing my magnesium intake, the anxiety and muscle spasms went away completely. The B-vitamins helped increase my energy and mood, and vitamin C helped me stay healthy.

It was good to feel better. I was gradually regaining more of my life.

CHAPTER 24

Supporting Families

I enjoyed my time as Middle School Director at our church. It allowed me to bring in extra income for our family, and I was still able to work with my kids.

In June, before Stephen started high school, I felt it was time to move on to something new. Once again, my heart was turned toward supporting foster and adoptive parents.

I became a Foster Parent Liaison through the Fostering Together program in Washington State. It was a government-funded program contracted through Olive Crest, a nonprofit that provides support to foster families.

My job was to recruit and support foster parents. I loved meeting and supporting people who were going through the licensing process, as well as those who were already licensed.

One day, a local foster parent contacted me. During the conversation, she mentioned another foster parent who was a mutual friend.

"How does she seem to have it all together, and I suck so badly at this parenting thing?" she asked me.

I laughed to myself. The foster parent she was referring to had called me the week before, telling me she was at the end of her rope.

I realized how easy it is to look at someone else and think they've got it together when we feel like a failure. I thought later about something Steven Furtick, author of *Unqualified*, said: "The reason we struggle with insecurity is because we compare our behind-the-scenes with everyone else's highlight reel."

During this time, I was asked to become a co-trainer for the state to train potential foster parents. I was also asked to speak and train for other programs, and I loved being able to share things I wished someone had told me in the beginning.

As I spoke to groups, I discovered overarching themes the families had in common. Many families were in crisis and struggling to find services to help their child. Most were feeling the same things I had throughout my journey. As I had been, they were afraid to admit it.

"In the beginning of your talk," one mom told me, "I was thinking, 'I can't believe she's sharing such strong emotions.' As the night went on, I realized I felt the exact same way."

One night while speaking to a group of foster parents at a local church, I asked them to brainstorm a list of emotions they'd experienced as a parent of a special needs child.

The emotions included confused, lost, unsure, frustrated, blessed, angry, sad, fearful, guilty, and bewildered. Some shared that they frequently felt like failures.

As the various groups worked on their lists, I overheard many parents exclaim, "Wow! I thought I was the only one who felt like that!" or "Hey! Me too!" Many said their emotions were so extreme they figured there was no way they could be normal feelings.

I told the parents something I'd often said to my kids: "Your emotions are a normal reaction to an abnormal situation."

I encouraged the parents to be honest. Pretending they were floating on a cotton-candy cloud riding a rainbow-colored unicorn, rather than acknowledging how angry they were, would not help their situation any more than it had helped mine.

As I learned to become gut-level honest with myself, I loved being able to give these parents a safe place to express themselves without fear of judgment or criticism.

Recognizing Progress

Stephen started high school in autumn. It was inspiring to watch him progress from not being able to read when he came to live with us, to reading a large textbook for college-level classes.

While he wasn't without struggles, his sense of compassion also amazed me. One Saturday, we had two young boys stay with us to give their foster mom a break. Stephen sat reading to the boys Dr. Seuss' *Green Eggs and Ham*, one of his favorite books for me to read to him when he was younger. As Stephen read, I marveled at how well he interacted with these children.

Stephen had spent the morning at the funeral of a kid from his class. Adam, who had been adopted from foster care the same year that Brianna and Stephen were, had slit his wrist only a couple of days earlier.

As I watched Stephen, I felt a sense of sadness for his friend's family, as well as relief to see him sitting there, alive, reading to these boys.

I teared up as I felt a swell of emotions and pride for all he had accomplished.

A few weeks later, I felt that same sense of pride as I shopped with Brianna. We were in American Eagle looking for school clothes, and it was actually fun to shop with her.

"I really want this vest," she said.

I looked at the price tag. "Now you know this vest is $60, right? You only have $100 left in your budget, so that wouldn't leave you with much."

"Oh, never mind then." She headed back to the clearance section, which she'd have rather died than do in the beginning.

Since Brianna liked expensive clothing, the previous year we'd started using a budget to make shopping a learning experience and not let it become another source of contention.

She insisted on wearing top-of-the line clothing and got only three outfits with the $250 we gave her. The first three days of school that year, she beamed as she left for school. She came back, bragging about how everyone loved her outfit.

On the fourth day, she got a few comments.

"Didn't you *just* wear that outfit?" a classmate had asked.

By the seventh and eighth day, everyone started to question her. "Don't you have any other clothes?"

Brianna got embarrassed.

I waited another week and then sat her down. "Brianna, I knew budgeting would be a tough skill to learn, so I set aside part of your school clothes money so you wouldn't spend it all on a few items. These clothes have to be long-sleeved so they go through winter, and you have $125 left. I'm going to take you shopping this weekend. I'd like you to think through what you need to buy."

I smiled to myself, noting how quickly she became frugal, heading back to the clearance racks right away as we entered the store.

At her next — and last — therapy appointment, I told her therapist how much fun it had been to shop with Bri. We'd been working with this therapist for years, and it was clear our time here was done. I felt both excitement and sadness over the thought of not driving four hours every other week to see her. We planned to find the kids a therapist closer to home if they felt they still needed support.

"When I tell you their progress is miraculous, I mean it," the therapist said. "I don't think you understand what I've been telling you. It is nothing short of a miracle. I've worked with kids like this for more than twenty years, and I've never seen a girl go from where your daughter started out to where she is now. Even with help, she should be cutting herself, suicidal, and running away. That she goes to her room when you tell her to is a miracle."

"Even with help this isn't normal?" I struggled to see how huge the kids' progress was, especially when we were still dealing with so many issues.

She leaned toward me, her gaze strong and direct, as if she were trying to get me to understand. "Even with the best of parents, this is amazing. Your kids have come far."

Her words made me realize that often I failed to recognize how far the kids had come, because I was focused on how far they still had to go. When my kids made a poor choice, despite all the emotional work we had done, I could still feel like a failure instead of realizing that their progress was nothing short of a miracle.

When I found myself getting frustrated with Parker's obnoxious antics, I had to remind myself that I didn't get one call that day from the school telling me to pick him up and I hadn't had to worry about him hurting our pets.

That was progress.

Riding the Waves

Brianna was always the kid who could bring me to the brink of insanity, causing me to want to strangle her one minute, and the next minute melt my heart. Just when I felt discouraged, she would write a sweet note or say something that helped me keep going.

On one of those weeks, the kids and I walked to the car with Bri's friend after church.

"Kayla, you should consider coming with us next week," I said as we walked toward the car.

Stephen jokingly piped in, "Don't listen to her. She gives bad advice."

As the rest of us laughed, Brianna's voice rose an octave as she exclaimed, "NO SHE DOESN'T! In fact, I don't know where I would be without her."

Her comment warmed my heart and renewed my desire to keep helping her heal. That glimmer may not have lasted an hour, but at that moment I knew the hard work was paying off, even though she often locked me out of her world so tightly it felt like I was hitting my head against a wall to reach her.

Later that year, Brianna had shown she could handle more freedom, so she had started working in the church nursery. Heidi, the Nursery Director, had become a dear friend over the past years. She knew about Brianna's struggles and was willing to keep an eye on her as she helped.

That fall, Maddie, another nursery worker, came to me and said, "I have to tell you what happened in the nursery today."

"What happened?" I was curious, unsure of whether to be scared or not.

"Heidi had paper leaves at the front desk of the nursery. People were supposed to write down what they were thankful for and tape them up on the wall. Brianna wrote 'Family' on hers."

"Really? That's so sweet."

"I know, I thought so too. In fact, as soon as she put it up on the wall, Heidi and I looked at each other and said, 'Awww!' The funny thing was she acted almost irritated with us. She looked at us like, 'Duh!' and said, 'Well, yeah, they saved me. Why shouldn't I be thankful?'"

"Wow! That's huge!"

"I know. I thought so too. I figured you'd love to know that."

After talking with Maddie, I thought back to an interesting conversation I'd had with Brianna the week before.

"My friends at school asked me today, 'What do you think your life would be like now if you'd never been adopted?'" she told me as she looked through the refrigerator to find an after-school snack.

"What did you tell them?" I asked, curious to hear what her answer had been.

"I told them I'd probably be a prostitute, on drugs, and on the streets." I guessed maybe she was right.

Both Brianna and Stephen, as they discovered how other kids from Place of Hope were faring, expressed gratitude. When they found out about Daniel, a boy they knew who'd joined a gang, Stephen told Lynn, "I am so thankful you guys adopted us. I think my life would be pretty messed up if you hadn't."

The summer before Parker turned eighteen, we had volunteered him to work in a camp for most of the summer. By the end of July, he had done such a good job that the camp director decided to pay him for the rest of the summer and give him back-pay for the month of June.

Dancing with a Porcupine

"Mom, I was so thankful you guys taught us to work hard," Parker said as he told me about the director's decision.

At the end of that summer, we had a neuropsychological evaluation done for him and discovered he was on the autism spectrum. That explained so much about his behavior over the years.

I thought about all the years of challenges and remembered an email I received one day. The email featured the most amazing shots of waves from the inside. This surfer evidently loved photography as well as surfing, thus earning him the title "Photographer of Surf." The pictures captured the most beautiful glimpses into what surfers see as they ride the wave.

I've always thought it would be fun to surf, but the chances of my tackling this sport were slim to none. I'd likely never see the inside of a wave up close, unlike those who brave the waves.

But here was a metaphor. While parenting wounded children felt like trying to stand in a monsoon, noticing those rare but divine moments made it more like "surfing the wave."

I had been hurt in the process, and sometimes it felt like I would drown in the overwhelming flood of emotions and issues, but I had the opportunity to witness God's transforming power in a way no one watching from shore would ever experience.

I had been able to see the amazing changes that take place as someone allows love to enter their heart. I had the privilege of watching a child's heart blossom and trust in a way that those on the outside will never even begin to understand. I knew how big those small steps of progress truly were.

I saw miraculous transformation in each of my kids' lives. Watching them grow and become who they truly are was incredibly rewarding, even though I couldn't always see the change taking place.

Just like the waves, sometimes those divine moments along the way didn't last long. I needed to enjoy them whenever they came and cherish them, much like a surfer rides a wave for a few moments.

One of those moments came on Mother's Day that year. Looking into my

Mother's Day basket, I was confused. Lynn and the kids told me this was a basket full of things I could use for my upcoming solitary writing retreat. Most of the items fit that theme: a candle, a soft blanket, at least three bars of dark chocolate, a journal, and a few bottles of scented bubble bath.

Among the sweet, little treasures, I noticed a bottle of whiskey and a flask that read, "Cheaper than therapy." I stared, trying to figure out what to think of it.

Stephen noticed that I was staring at the flask. His eyes twinkled mischievously, and he grinned from ear to ear.

"I convinced Dad to let me buy that for you!"

I laughed. "I'm so confused, Stephen. You know I don't drink, so why this?"

"Because, Mom. With all you've gone through with us I don't know how we haven't driven you to drinking yet!"

I laughed. How vastly different this Mother's Day was from those of previous years! Even Parker was excited to give me a gift and had helped pick out some of the items.

I didn't tell Stephen that I was as surprised as he was.

New Directions

I raced around the house, cleaning in preparation for my parents' arrival, as well as for the party guests who'd be coming that Saturday. While I tidied up the apartment-sized guest house we had renovated next to our garage, I looked over the "Owens" wall we'd created in the small living room. Large letters bearing our last name hung there, as well as pictures in a fun, whimsical assortment of frames we had plastered on the wall.

I stopped and smiled as I thought back to the moments captured within the frames. As the kids grew and matured, we experienced more of the enjoyable parts of parenting, including traveling more, which Lynn and I loved.

I looked over years of trips to Seaside, Wallowa Lake, and other extended family vacations. A stop at Dave and Busters on the way home from my parents' house in Wisconsin at Christmas hung there, along with stops to see Old Faithful and Mount Rushmore on the way to South Dakota the summers that Lynn and I led family mission trips for our church.

The second summer we took families to South Dakota to do mission work, we also took Dustin, a teenager who worked as a leader in the middle school ministry with me. Neither of his parents were able to attend, so we "adopted" him into the Owens clan for the week, and he had remained part of the family ever since that summer.

I noted Dustin's tall stature, his bright, blue eyes, and blond hair on several of the pictures. Now 21, he not only took other trips with us, but he had become like a son. I thoroughly enjoyed the relationship Lynn and I had developed with him.

My eyes rested on a picture from the summer before Brianna's senior year when

Dustin went with us to Indiana. We drove there for a family reunion on my mom's side. The kids had made such huge strides that I'd felt a surge of pride as I introduced them to my extended family.

On the way back, Lynn and I had also enjoyed introducing the kids to one of our favorite places in the world – Chicago. We dragged them to classic places like Sears Tower (Lynn and I refuse to call it the Willis Tower), Navy Pier, Millennium Park, and Ed Debevics, and introduced them to the wonder called Chicago-style pizza. While I savored the deep-dish pizza, they wrote their names on the wall of Gino's restaurant.

As I looked back at the pictures from Chicago, my heart sank. It was the last trip we took with the kids before Brianna moved out, just months before she would have graduated. I held back tears as I thought about how she still hadn't made any effort to finish high school, even though she would soon be 21 and would have no option but a GED.

We knew she was couch-surfing and going from one unhealthy relationship to another, and she was involved in other unhealthy activities as well.

As I dried my tears and began dusting, my eyes rested on another picture. The sweet face of a two-and-a-half-year-old boy looked back at me, a face I'd smothered with kisses over the past month and a half. Sebastian, a young boy we had been approached about adopting, had given me more love in those past couple of months than I'd experienced from all three of the other kids in ten years.

Despite his short time in our family, this little boy ran toward me, squealing with glee and delight, after I had been gone for only a couple hours. He loved to snuggle and hug, and though he'd experienced trauma of his own during his short life thus far, he had already healed so much.

As I experienced the beautiful process of attachment with this little boy, I realized that all relationships involve a dance. When your partner works with you, the movements flow, and it doesn't feel like work. You have fun. But it's hard to dance with someone who is stepping on your feet, pushing you away, or kicking you in the knee, even if you know they're doing it out of fear.

I noted more pictures. There was Brianna's prom picture during her junior year, as well as a picture of her and Lynn all dolled up for the annual Father-Daughter

Ball. I chuckled as I thought back to the first one they'd attended.

I saw the picture of Stephen's track meet and the one we had taken with him standing in front of the '68 Mustang that he and Lynn were restoring.

In another picture, Parker stood with his friends after the announcement that their Destination Imagination team had made it to Nationals in Nashville, TN.

As I thought back to his first day in a school behavioral program, when he was more interested in looking for rocks than making friends, I realized that it marked a huge accomplishment. Not only did he now have a wonderful group of friends, but they had also worked together to overcome the DI collaborative problem-solving challenges to achieve that goal.

Parker was about to add another, more significant, accomplishment: graduation. As I thought back over the previous ten years, I found it hard to believe that this day had come. At one time, he caused chaos in five classrooms around him. Even in his freshman year of high school, he needed a one-on-one para educator by his side to make it through a school day.

Now he was about to graduate after a year of all A's and B's. The following fall, he planned to attend Gather 4 Him, a small Christian college. He had even applied for college and financial aid without prompting. Not only was it a huge accomplishment for him, but for Lynn and I as well, with the vast amount of work we had invested to help him get to this point.

Lynn and I had accomplished a few things of our own.

Lynn had graduated with his Master's in counseling and developed a thriving counseling practice that could barely keep up with the demand, despite constantly adding and training more therapists.

I had turned my focus toward our nonprofit organization, Forever Homes. We provided multiple locations for Rejuvenate Retreat, which we developed to pamper and support foster and adoptive moms and to connect them to each other and to local resources.

Lynn and I also continued to speak and provide training, and I was still contracted with the state to train potential foster parents in our area.

I've heard it said that "God often uses our deepest pain as the launching pad of our greatest calling."

I fully believe that to be true.

Final Word... For Now

God has used our painful journey to help more foster and adoptive parents than we could have imagined. More than just helping others, God has used our journey to make some needed changes in my heart and give me hope that, despite how difficult or dark circumstances seem, He is working behind the scenes for my good and the good of those around me.

If you picked up this book to read because you are fostering or have adopted a child with serious challenges – bless you! I pray you are encouraged to believe that you will survive this, that good — far greater than you can imagine — will come from your commitment to extraordinary love. Your sacrifice and all it has cost you is not in vain.

If you picked up this book to read because someone you know is fostering or has adopted a child with serious challenges – bless you! I pray that you are better equipped to intelligently and compassionately help and encourage them. Please remember that they likely don't need your input as much as they need your ear. You might be the only one who has listened to them in years.

If you picked up this book to read for some other reason – or maybe don't even know why you did – bless you, too. God has a reason to have you walk through this story with us, and I trust that you will someday know why, and that you will be a little better prepared for it because you took the time to read this.

None of our experiences were wasted. Every struggle, every pain, every difficulty has been used for God's glory and our good. I do not want to go back and relive what we have been through, but God used it all to grow me – and us – in ways I never thought possible.

I can tell you from my heart that I cannot wait to see what He has for us next!

CPSIA information can be obtained
at www.ICGtesting.com
Printed in the USA
BVHW051303091221
623633BV00009B/433

9 780692 831847